Multiple and Intersecting Identities in Qualitative Research

Multiple and Intersecting Identities in Qualitative Research

Edited by

Betty M. Merchant
Arlette Ingram Willis
University of Illinois at Urbana-Champaign

2001

LAWRENCE ERLBAUM ASSOCIATES, PUBLISHERS
Mahwah, New Jersey   London

Lawrence Erlbaum Associates, Inc., Publishers
10 Industrial Avenue
Mahwah, NJ 07430

Cover design by Kathryn Houghtaling Lacey

Library of Congress Cataloging-in-Publication Data

Multiple and intersecting identities in qualitative
   research
            p. cm.
      Includes bibliographical references and index.
ISBN 0-8058-2874-5 (cloth : alk. paper) — ISBN
   0-8058-2875-3 (pbk. : alk. paper)
1. Education—Research—Social aspects—United States
   2. Qualitative research—United States—. 3. Women in
   education—United States. 4. Multicultural education—United States. 5. Educational anthropology—
   United States. I. Merchant, Betty M. II. Willis, Arlett
   Ingram.
   LB1028.25.U6 S65 2000
370'.7'2—dc21
                                                    99-059086
                                                         CIP

Printed in the United States of America
10 9 8 7 6 5 4 3 2 1

To my mother, Lucille Merchant, who taught me how to wrestle with a problem until I solved it, and to the memory of my father, Earl Merchant, who taught me how to listen, observe and appreciate the world around me.

–Betty M. Merchant

To my mother, Angie White Ingram, and aunt, Willa White Williams, whose love and understanding daily bless my life.

–Arlette Ingram Willis

Contents

Preface

This book is a collection of reflections of researchers as they have attempted to analyze the personal and professional context in which their research was conducted. As women researchers, young in our professional lives, we argue that our gender, race, religion, and status have played a significant role in our research agendas. As women researchers, we offer a female perspective, though not a feminist critique, per se, for we believe that our gender does play a significant role in our research efforts. In addition, race, religion, and class, whether as women of color or a White woman conducting research among people of color, has played a significant role in our research. Our unique positionality allows us to understand relationships across many boundaries.

We have found that in most cases, because of our position as women and/or people of color, we have not had some of the traditional problems associated with access to the culturally specific settings. We have, however, encountered a number of other issues, and in this book, we share how, as researchers, we have met and resolved these issues for our particular settings. Moreover, each chapter author discusses how, in addressing these issues, she labored to meet the standards of academia, often at a personal cost.

OVERVIEW

Betty Merchant's chapter "pairs" with Martha Zurita's, in the sense that the two chapters present their contrasting perspectives of a study of limited- and non-English speaking students, in which they attempted to collaborate with one another. In chapter 1, Betty Merchant focuses on the complex issues that arose while she, as a White researcher, supervised Martha Zurita, a Mexican-American graduate student who was assisting her in studying the schooling experiences of newly arrived Mexican immigrants at a rural high school in which all but one of the educators were White. Martha Zurita, in chapter 2, focuses on her commitment to action research and on her personal frustration with a repressive educational system in which many of the Mexican students were experiencing social and academic difficulties that were similar to those that she and members of her own family had experienced in high school.

In chapter 6, Beloo Mehra explores the implications of being both an "insider" and an "outsider" with respect to the Asian Indian families she was studying, and the ways in which these overlapping but incongruent identities shaped her actions as she conducted her dissertation research. Lubna Chaudhry, in chapter 3, writes about how Islam has shaped the ways in which she conceptualizes and implements research among people who have a very traditional view of how Pakistani women should behave. In so doing, she provides us with a fascinating look at the intersection of ethnicity, religion, culture, and gender.

In chapter 4, Arlette Ingram Willis calls attention to the ways in which dissenting voices are excluded from mainstream dialogues, and powerfully illustrates the dilemmas she faces as an African American woman and researcher. Annette Henry, in chapter 5, illustrates the inadequacies inherent in simple definitions of identity and positionality, as she discusses her African and Caribbean roots and the ways in which these affect the kind of research she undertakes.

In chapter 7, Anya Enos weaves her story in the tradition of a Native American craftswoman and provides us with considerable insight into her dilemmas as a Native American woman, rejecting traditional models of research that have wreaked considerable damage on Native populations. She attempts to design and implement a methodology that is compatible with the Native community and culture. In chapter 8 Judy Kim also points to the inadequacy of cultural labels by questioning the different meanings associated with what it means to be a Korean. Her chapter also probes the extent of her credibility as an American-born Korean, studying Korean nationals.

Taken as a whole, these seven chapters offer a serious challenge to the overly simplistic, often dichotomous descriptors (e.g., "insider" versus "outsider") that have dominated the research literature for far too long. The authors write directly and courageously about the ways in which their multiple identities and positionalities harmonize, and at times conflict, with those of their research participants; in doing so, they call attention to important complexities in the qualitative research process that have, until now, received little or no attention.

We make no apologies for bringing to the table ways of knowing that are not part of the mainstream of academic life. We are not constrained by these ways of knowing, but believe they have aided us in understanding specific cultural, linguistic, gendered, and religious points of view that have failed to become a part of the mainstream.

ACKNOWLEDGMENTS

I thank Martha Zurita, Beloo Mehra, and Edith Cisneros for agreeing to be my research assistants, for being courageous enough to be reflective about the research endeavors in which we were engaged, and for being intellectually honest and caring enough to share their insights with me. It is they who provided me with my first genuine experience of collaboration, and they who directed my attention to the importance of providing a forum for discussing the issues presented in this book. I also thank my son, Damon, and my daughter, Danica, for being patient and supportive of me, even when the time I spent working on this book meant taking valuable time away from them. Lastly, I express my heartfelt appreciation to Shirley Fryer and Diana Whitt, who have sustained me personally and professionally since my arrival at the University of Illinois, and who provided unconditional support for this endeavor.

—*Betty M. Merchant*

I extend my sincere thanks to my graduate student Karla C. Lewis for her support, efficiency, and friendship. A note of thanks is also extended to Patricia James for her many hours of clerical support with this project.

A heartfelt thank-you to my foremothers and mentors who have worked tirelessly, with little hope of reward, so that I can realize my dreams. Finally, a special thanks to my husband, Leonard, and my sons, Lenny, Justin, and Jacob, for the loving kindness they extend to me daily.

—*Arlette Ingram Willis*

Introduction

We invite you to learn of the songs of our souls—for recalling the past, altering the present, and transforming the future. In this book, we become the subjects of our own lives and research within and outside of the academy. Extending our sense of time and space, we acknowledge that our current status is the result of "collective struggle and support. Thus our understanding of our roles includes an interweaving of the personal and the public—the intellectual and the emotional—the scholarly and the political" (Ladson-Billings, 1996, p. 59). We are not the first group of women to write about our experiences as educational researchers, nor are we attempting to represent a monolithic view of women, especially women of color, who conduct qualitative research among members of their own communities. We are seeking to extend the current discourse on the role of cultural knowledge in qualitative research, especially research conducted by women of color within their community. Through self-reflection we try "telling the past as we have learned it, mouth-to-mouth, telling the present as we see, know, and feel it in our hearts and with our words" (hooks, 1989, p.3).

In this book, the chapters detail growth and struggle, joy and pain, fear and confusion, worry and doubt, as each researcher attempts to conceptualize herself as a researcher, at the same time trying to honor her cultural connectedness and knowledge. Not surprisingly, each author has carved out her own distinct pathway to arrive at her present understanding of what it means to be a woman who conducts research within her own community. In order to develop these understandings, each woman testifies to the unsettledness she has experienced. Thus, there are multiple dimensions of complexity reflected in each chapter that acknowledge and try to convey how conscious and unconscious cultural knowledge and memory help to inform her research in substantive and powerful ways.

The wholeness of our lives as women and researchers of color, who conduct research within our own communities, forms the heart of this work. We do not see ourselves solely within categories of race, gender, class, language, and religion because these categories occur simultaneously within our lives, nudging and intersecting, shaping and reshaping our realities.

It is customary in scholarly works to share with the readers the conceptual frame of reference of the editors/authors. This task has been especially difficult, as the theories that focus on race and those espoused by women of color are often marginalized within the academy and their authors become of light worth. Nor do the theories driving this work fit neatly into the categories of feminism, womanism, critical race theory, etc. The theories, paradigms, and methods that undergird mainstream research, the "master's tools," to borrow a phrase from Lorde (1984), do not work especially well for us either. For we maintain that is imperative that we remain grounded in our own cultural and gendered ways of knowing. Yet, we are aware that when a person of color conducts research among her own, it never fails to appear questionable to many. As Trinh (1987) wrote "The question concerning the choice of subject matter immediately arises, sometimes out of curiosity, most often out of hostility. The marriage is not consumable, for the pair is no longer outside/inside, that is to say, objective versus subjective, but something between inside/inside—objective in what is already claimed as objective" (p. 374). At some point, we are both inside and outside within our communities and within the academy. This prompts the question: Where does this research fit? We see it most closely aligned to the research and literature of other women of color who conduct research in their own communities (Delgato-Gaitain, 1997; Ladson-Billings, 1994, 1996; and Villenas, 1996 to name a few). One will find that

> the once dominant ideal of a detached observer using neutral language to explain "raw" data has been displaced by an alternative project that attempts to understand human conduct as it unfolds through time and in relation to its meaning for the actor. (Rosaldo, 1989, p. 37)

Moreover, we acknowledge ourselves and our position within our multiple communities, attempting to use compassionate language as we delve into the ethnomethodological issues that beset us while conducting our research.

Multiple and Intersecting Identities in Qualitative Research is a compilation of the work of several women researchers who agreeably are challenged by the possibility of using narratives to illustrate how culture actively informs their lives as researchers. Thompson's (1998) description of the moral power of narrative is worth quoting at length. She writes that in this sense *story* "is a matter of creatively reshaping experience so that what is revealed is not simply what is already known, but rather what is there but not understood. Here, the emphasis is less on the readily recognizable 'Aha!' moments than on providing a rich, complex, and nuanced story that captures more than the eye can see, thus giving the reader or listener insight into the as yet not fully known. This sort of story teaches the reader or listener how to read, how to see or hear; it does not show things as literal truths, but calls upon the reader to engage in the process of meaning-making and interpretation," (Thompson, 1998, p. 538).

The views of the authors contributing to this book serve as a parallax from which to view the context and text of their lives and research. Trinh (1987) has observed:

> the moment the insider steps out from the inside she's no longer a mere insider. She necessarily looks in from the outside while also looking out from the inside. Not quite the same, not quite the other, she stands in that undetermined threshold place where she constantly drifts in and out. (p. 374)

Significantly, the authors attempt to note the points of intersection and digression between their lived experiences, cultural knowledge, and academic ways of knowing. Cynthia Tyson (1998) observes that "these intersections demand that we not only look at theories, methodologies, and epistemologies, but that we endeavor to uplift as we inquire" (p. 22). Paradoxically, in sharing the narratives and metanarratives, we have transformed the very realities we wish to share and we are transformed as well. As a result, we all are differently informed about ourselves and our communities. In this ethereal context, each researcher uses metanarratives that exist within her frames of reference. Trinh (1987) notes that "differences do not exist only between outsider and insider—two entities. They are also at work within the outsider herself, or the insider herself—single entity. She knows she cannot speak of *them* without speaking of herself, of *history* without involving her story, also that she cannot make a gesture without activating the to-and-fro movement of life (p. 375).

Sonja Sanchez (1998) calls us to "come with yourselves, singing life, singing eyes, singing hands, alarming the death singers, that you have come to celebrate life, until we become seeing men and women again". We invite you to come learn of our songs, songs of our souls recalling the past, filling the present, and believing in the future.

—*Arlette Ingram Willis*
Betty M. Merchant

REFERENCES

Delagto-Gaitan, C. (1997). Dismantling borders. In A. Neumann & P. Peterson (Eds.), *Learning from our lives: Women, research, and autobiography in education*, (pp. 37–51). New York: Teachers College Press

hooks, B. (1989). *Talking back: Thinking feminist thinking black*. Boston: South End Press.

Ladson-Billings, G. (1994). *The dreamkeepers: Successful teachers of African American children*. San Francisco, CA: Jossey-Bass.

Ladson-Billings, G. (1996). Lifting as we climb: The womanist tradition in multicultural education. In J. Banks (Ed.), *Multicultural education, transformative knowledge, and action*. New York: Teachers College Press.

Lorde, A. *Sister Outsider*. Trumansberg, NY: The Crossing Press.

Rosaldo, R. (1989). *Culture and truth: The remaking of social analysis*. Boston: Beacon.

Sanchez, S. (1998). Commencement address. http://www.temple.edu/EOP/commencementnt98/Sanchez.html

Thompson, A. (1998). Not the color purple: Black feminist lessons for educational caring. *Harvard Educational Review, 68*(4), 522–554.

Trinh, M. (1990). Not you/like you: Post-colonial women and the interlocking questions of identity and difference. In G. Anzaldua, (Ed.), *Making face, making soul: Creative and critical perspectives of feminists of color* (pp. 371–375), San Francisco: Spinters/Aunt Lute Books.

Tyson, C. (1998). A response to "Coloring epistemologies: Are our qualitative research epistemologies racially biased?" Educational Researcher, 27(9), 21–22.

Villenas, S (1996). The colonizer/colonized Chicana ethnographer: Identity, marginalization, and co-optation in the field. *Harvard Educational Review, 64*(4), 711–731.

1

Negotiating the Boundaries and Sometimes Missing the Mark: A White Researcher and a Mexican American Research Assistant

Betty M. Merchant
University of Illinois–Urbana–Champaign

Martha and I were introduced to each other in 1992, through the Summer Research Opportunities Program (SROP), which provides an opportunity for talented students to pursue a research topic of interest to them, aided by a faculty member of their choice. Martha approached me at the suggestion of a colleague who was familiar with my work. According to SROP guidelines, the prospective faculty–student pair introduce themselves to one another, and on the basis of their initial conversation, decide whether they will work together. Our first meeting was a positive one; and consistent with the spirit of SROP, our interactions that summer focused on Martha's research objectives and the ways in which I could help her achieve those objectives. In the years that followed, Martha and I developed a close personal relationship. Over time, the trust and compassion that grew out of our interactions permitted us a space in which to examine the ways in which our differing ethnicities, subjectivities, positionalities, and views of research resulted in our sometimes missing the mark with each other as we attempted to engage in collaborative research efforts.

Expanding Our Collaboration

Martha and I worked together in the SROP the following summer as well; that summer, her research focused on course taking patterns of Latino undergraduates at the University of Illinois. From 1994 to 1996, Martha and I continued to collaborate in conjunction with a university assistantship awarded to her for working with a faculty member of her own choosing.

In the first year, our work focused on the research issues with which I was concerned. In the second year, we began to examine some of the issues that had emerged during the first year of fieldwork in the school. Most notably, Martha was becoming increasingly upset about the ways in which some of the district- and building-level policies and the teacher and administrator practices, which we had identified the previous year, were contributing to the academic and social marginalization of the Mexican students. Although I was deeply concerned about the school's lack of responsiveness to the needs of these students, I viewed the situation through the eyes of a White researcher whose access to the school was undoubtedly facilitated by the fact that the superintendent, principal, and teachers were also White. Martha, on the other hand, as a member of the subordinated group, had spent an entire school year observing the processes of subjugation that she, her family, and friends had experienced in schools.

Whereas I observed the inequitable treatment of the Mexican students and sought a way of using our research to transform policy and practice among teachers and administrators—the power elites, of which I was a member—the ethnic group that was being systematically disadvantaged by the educators in the school was the group to which Martha belonged; her outrage was something I could only partly understand. As a doctoral student who had invested so much of her life in the educational system, she understood all too well the long-term consequences of the academic failure of the Mexican students in the school. As a member of the group that was being marginalized, Martha did not believe that either the teachers or administrators were genuinely interested in improving the conditions of the Mexican students in the school, so she directed her attention to exploring ways in which Latina/Latino graduate students from the university could provide direct instructional services to the struggling high school students.

The 2 years that Martha and I spent conducting fieldwork in Agriville (pseudonym) raised a number of critical issues; a few of these were common to both of us, but for the most part, the research process was experienced and interpreted very differently by each of us. Martha's and my chapters were written as companion pieces in an effort to make explicit, to ourselves and to others, the ways in which our respective—and previously unexamined—positionalities and subjectivities were enacted within the research setting. This process of critical self-reflection has not been an enjoyable one; it has, among other things, interrupted my complacency, challenged my self-image, and, at times, disrupted my interactions with friends and colleagues as I sought to understand my actions through their eyes. To interrogate myself is to feel frustrated, angry, isolated, vulnerable, foolish, and, at times, immobilized in the eye of a storm; it is also to feel compassion for myself and those with whom I interact, as I seek to identify and describe the inequities in our society, to examine my role in maintaining these inequities, and to collaborate with others on eradicating them.

Unpacking Martha's and My Relationship

When we began working together, some of the differences between us were quite obvious. Martha's parents emigrated from Mexico to Illinois and raised their children in the city of Chicago. Although my grandparents emigrated from Canada, my parents were born in the United States and brought up their children in a small village in rural northeastern New York State. Whereas Spanish was the primary language used in Martha's home as she was growing up, English was the dominant language in my household. When we conducted the research project that is the subject of this chapter, Martha was a doctoral student and I was an assistant professor in the university. As such, I enjoyed a higher level of income and greater status in the institution than she did. Having enrolled in a doctoral program immediately after receiving her undergraduate degree, Martha was relatively young when we worked in Agriville. In fact, she was frequently mistaken for a student, and some of the students thought that I was her mother.

The differences between Martha and me are numerous, and significantly influenced not only what we experienced in Agriville Junior/Senior High School, but how we reacted to those experiences and to one another. In addition to the differences, however, there are also some parallels between our lives, although they are less obvious, I believe that they have helped us to sustain a positive relationship with one another over the years. Both Martha and I grew up in blue-collar, Roman Catholic families whose parents' linguistic traditions were not English (my mother was a monolingual French speaker when she started school). Both Martha and I were identified as able students who experienced a considerable amount of success within the educational system. Although all of my five siblings and two of Martha's six brothers and sisters have graduated from college, she and I were the first ones in our families to pursue doctoral degrees.

In a number of ways, Martha and I chose to pursue paths that differ markedly from that of our family members. As a consequence of these choices, we have both endured criticisms and concerns that spring from our family's fears that we have chosen a lifestyle that is too stress filled, complex, and too far away from the kind of life we were brought up to lead. The sense of marginality and professional vulnerability that is associated with pursuing a career that differs markedly from the expectations and lifestyles of the other members of our families is one that Martha and I both share, although her decision to pursue an academic career has generated much more anxiety for her mother than for mine.

Our personalities are also similar in some respects: We take pride in the fact that we have overcome a number of obstacles to gain access to opportunities that would otherwise have been denied to us; we tend to meet life head on with enthusiasm; and we are passionate about many of the same issues.

My perception of the similarities between us tended to obscure important differences between us, which prevented me from realizing that we were experiencing the process very differently from each other. There were a number of other factors that also got in the way of my understanding the discomfort and anger Martha experienced while conducting the Agriville study. Coming of age in the 1960s, I had, over the years, come to view myself as liberal and open-minded—an advocate for equity and justice. Even when Martha attempted to communicate some of her frustrations to me, I assured myself that I was a good listener and a compassionate person. As a consequence, I allowed myself to be seduced into believing that Martha and I experienced the research process in much the same way and that I was responding adequately to her needs and concerns. For example, in the rural high school where we were conducting our research, Martha and I observed that the majority of Mexican students were marginalized by their teachers and non-Mexican peers. Although I commiserated with Martha over this, I failed to address the fact that the situations we observed held very different meanings and implications for Martha, whose ethnicity was the same as these students and whose previous schooling experiences had often been similarly hurtful.

MARTHA AND ME AND OUR STUDY OF MEXICAN IMMIGRANTS IN A RURAL ILLINOIS HIGH SCHOOL

Martha, Me, and the School Personnel

When we went into the school to conduct our fieldwork, Martha expected that I, rather than she, would interview the administrators and teachers because I was the faculty member overseeing the study and she was my research assistant. When it came to the students, however, Martha felt confident about assuming the major responsibility for initiating conversations with them in order to gain a better understanding of their schooling experiences.

Because I am a Euro-American, the teachers saw me as "one of them," whereas they construed Martha's ethnicity as oppositional to theirs. The extent to which ethnic subjectivities conditioned not only the teachers' and administrators' responses to Martha and me, but our interactions with them, was complicated by the fact that our study focused on the experiences of newly immigrated, limited- and non-English-speaking Mexican students in the school.

Although my initial interactions with the teachers were undoubtedly facilitated by the fact that we all belonged to the same general ethnic group, there were other aspects of my identity that played an important role in their acceptance of me. I taught in K–12 classrooms for 16 years prior to becoming a university professor, and I was the same age as the majority of teachers in Agriville Junior/Senior High School. I also grew up in a small rural town very much like Agriville in size and socioeconomic status, populated by lower- to-middle-class farmers and railroad workers. As a young doctoral student from Chicago who had never been a classroom teacher, Martha found that none of her multiple identities meshed very well with those of the Agriville teachers.

As a consequence, Martha tried to avoid the teachers' lounge because she felt that faculty members were uncomfortable around her and either didn't know what to say or carefully monitored their interactions with her in order to present themselves as politically correct. The conversations she did have with the teachers focused on their concerns about the Mexican students, particularly concerns that related to discipline problems. When some of these teachers sought Martha's advice about what to do with the students, she felt uncomfortable being designated as the "Mexican expert" and did not want to play a major role in advising teachers. She believed that if her suggestions to teachers did not work out, they would either blame her or the Mexican students rather than look for alternative explanations. As the academic year progressed, teachers increasingly called on Martha to tutor the limited- and non-English-speaking Mexican students in their classrooms; she came to resent this expectation and viewed this as an abdication of their responsibility for educating the Mexican students. She also felt that these requests for tutoring trivialized or ignored her role as researcher in the school.

Toward the end of the year, some of the Agriville teachers became convinced that the increase in behavioral problems that was occurring among the Mexican students was a direct result of Martha's interactions with these students. More interesting, the only teachers who approached me directly were the Spanish teacher and the bilingual education teacher who, until Martha arrived, were the only Spanish-speaking educators in the school. Their specific concern was that Martha's presence in the school was contributing to the undesirable "empowerment" of the Mexican immigrants. Both teachers associated the increase in discipline problems among these students with their closeness to Martha and their tendency to confide in her.

The Spanish teacher did not voice concerns about Martha until after a conversation in which Martha criticized her teaching methods. Following that conversation, the teacher began to describe to me incidents in which students were seen giving notes to Martha—notes that she believed were critical of the teachers in the school and of a conspiratorial nature. I discussed the accusations with Martha and she assured me that the notes the students had given her were just the ordinary teenagers' notes about their social lives; but I was never able to convince the Spanish teacher that this had been the case.

I believe that the bilingual education teacher, although extremely uncomfortable around me, was particularly threatened by Martha and that this accounted for her refusal to let either of us observe her classroom instruction. (Unlike Martha, however, I was permitted to interview her on several occasions.) Some of the factors contributing to her discomfort with Martha undoubtedly included the fact that the bilingual education teacher was White, as well as the fact that Martha's ability to speak Spanish meant that she could understand and critique the verbal interaction between the teacher and the Mexican students. Because Martha's undergraduate training was in mathematics and she possessed considerably more expertise in this content area than did the bilingual teacher, she was able to detect and correct the many errors in algebra homework that the Mexican students had completed under the bilingual teacher's tutelage. Martha's rapport with the Mexican students posed a threat to the almost exclusive relationship the bilingual education teacher had enjoyed with them as a result of the other teachers' inability to speak Spanish.

Martha and Me and the Mexican Students

I depended on Martha to speak with the Mexican students in Spanish and to ask them the questions I had framed, as well as to modify these questions and introduce others she felt were appropriate. The Mexican students and their families immediately recognized Martha as one of them. Although the students could see that I was not Mexican, they initially thought that Martha and I had come to the school together because she was my daughter and I was enrolling her as a high school student.

The enthusiasm with which the Mexican students first greeted Martha diminished somewhat over the course of the 2 years we worked in the high school. For the first several months of our study, these students would flock to her like the Pied Piper, greeting her enthusiastically, chatting with her about the latest gossip, and requesting her assistance with their homework in various subjects. On the days I would come to the school alone, the students would always ask whether or not Martha had also come; when they learned she had not, they became silent, turned, and walked away. Such incidents made it apparent that the Mexican students enjoyed a special relationship with Martha that they did not share with me—a non-Spanish speaking, middle-aged, White university researcher. Given this, it is clear that without Martha's help, I could not have learned what I did about the students, their families, or their schooling experiences in Agriville.

Despite the fact that Martha's interactions with the students provided valuable information that was beneficial to me, these interactions proved costly to her. Although she was initially responsive to the students' requests for help with their school assignments, Martha eventually stopped providing these services. There were several reasons for this. Over time, she began to feel that the students were becoming more interested in receiving the answers from her than in learning the process by which they could arrive at the answers themselves; they were also frequently noisy and disruptive during her tutorial sessions in the study hall. Another reason Martha decided to discontinue tutoring was that she became increasingly frustrated with what she perceived as a patchwork approach to schooling the Mexican students. She believed that the Mexican students really needed bilingual, content-based classes, and that anything short of this was insufficient. She felt her tutoring was not meeting the educational needs of the students and she no longer wanted to participate in something she did not believe had any real impact on their learning. As the months went by, Martha became less and less comfortable in the school; she felt marginalized and devalued in an environment that was hostile to her presence.

Although Martha was less than enthusiastic about spending time in the school, I encouraged her to focus on the few teachers who were trying to engage her in conversations during her visits to the school. I also advised her to stop tutoring the Mexican students because I could see that she felt enormous pressure to fill the gaps between what newly immigrated, limited- and non-English speaking Mexican students were able to accomplish and what their teachers expected of them.

Martha's increasing frustration with the school's unresponsiveness to the needs of these students emerged as a significant issue in our research. At first, I believed that I could empathize with her feelings in this regard. I was also becoming increasingly upset at the trajectory of failure that characterized the social behavior and academic performance of many of the Mexican students we were observing—a trajectory that too many of the teachers appeared to accept as inevitable, and one that the students themselves began to accept over time. It was not until Martha and I were several months into the study that I realized that, after spending a full day in the school, we generally experienced severe headaches on the ride back to campus; and we often took naps as soon as we arrived at our respective homes because we felt so emotionally drained by the experience. Although I knew that Martha was having a difficult time participating in the study, not until many months into the academic year did I fully realize how much more stressful the project was for her than for me. At that point, I acknowledged Martha's request to disassociate herself from the school site and encouraged her to engage in other research-related studies on campus—such as extending the literature review and transcribing our earlier field notes. On those occasions when Martha did accompany me to the school, I shortened our observations to half days, and this seemed to relieve the stress for both of us.

When Martha told the students that she would no longer provide tutorial services, several of them appeared disappointed and upset and pulled back from her. Although this decision created some distance between Martha and some of the Mexican students, her frustrations at trying to work with them unexpectedly resulted in some of the teachers feeling closer to her because they saw her as experiencing some of same difficulties they had encountered in trying to teach these students. Being perceived by the teachers as more teacher-friendly and less student-friendly was not comforting to Martha, however.

ISSUES EMERGING FROM MY CONDUCTING RESEARCH WITH MARTHA ON MEXICAN IMMIGRANTS IN A RURAL ILLINOIS HIGH SCHOOL

Martha's Identification with the Marginalized Students

In participating in this study, Martha found that she identified with the Mexican high school students and their families on a number of levels. Her mother emigrated from Mexico, works in a factory, and still struggles with the English language; the majority of the students' parents work in local factories and have limited proficiency in English. Despite the fact that she is now an American citizen, Martha's mother is periodically harassed by agents from the Immigration and Naturalization Services who "raid" the factory in which she works in order to identify and seize undocumented immigrants; a number of the students in the high school and their families are undocumented.

Martha was identified as an academically gifted student throughout the years she attended Chicago's public schools, yet during those years she became keenly aware of the ways in which teachers and principals marginalized not only her but other Mexican students and their parents, most notably those who were poor and had difficulty speaking English. Because of her desire to improve the conditions of schooling for Mexican students, Martha once thought about becoming a high school mathematics teacher. She eventually abandoned the idea of obtaining a teaching credential and graduated from the University of Illinois with a bachelor's degree in mathematics. Toward the end of her undergraduate years, her interests shifted from participating in the system as a classroom teacher to conducting research on the ways in which particular educational policies and practices contribute to the exclusion of specific groups of students within the schools.

Although Martha's identification with the Mexican students helped her move easily among them, this identification also presented difficulties for her. Because she saw herself as having come from a background similar to theirs, she found herself extremely upset with students she perceived as unwilling to exert a reasonable effort in their studies. In addition, Martha found herself comparing some of the students with other people she knew, and predicting certain outcomes for the students based on her knowledge of friends and relatives who manifested similar behaviors in their youth.

Martha empathized with the Mexican students in a way that I, as a White, middle-class university researcher could not. Nonetheless, I was very concerned about the difficulties these students were experiencing with their teachers and their White peers.

My Shifting Stance With Respect to the Agriville Teachers

My 16 years of teaching elementary and high school students who were classified as poor, minority, and having special needs contributed to my lack of tolerance for much of what I observed happening between Agriville educators and the Mexican students. In the first few months of the study, I had no difficulty identifying the victims (the Mexican students) and the perpetrators (the principal and the majority of the classroom teachers). When sharing drafts of my impressions of the first few months of fieldwork in Agriville with several friends and colleagues, I was told, however, that my research had taken on an "administrator- and teacher-bashing" aspect; some of the strongest objections came from a Mexican American colleague. In reflecting on the merits of this criticism, I realized that I had focused almost exclusively on the students' schooling experiences and their interpretations of these experiences, but had remained relatively inattentive to the teachers' and principal's perspectives regarding their interactions with these students.

Because the teachers appeared to be uncomfortable talking to Martha about their experiences with the Mexican students and I was unable to speak to these students in Spanish, I decided, in the second half of the study, that I should put more effort into learning about the teachers' and principal's perspectives while Martha focused her energies on understanding and representing the experiences of the Mexican students. On the one hand, this division of labor was reasonable, given Martha's and my differential access to the faculty and student groups. On the other hand, the differentiation of tasks made it seem, at times, as if I were becoming more sympathetic to the teachers and principal, "taking sides" with them against the Mexican students (and, at times, Martha).

Research for Understanding Versus Advocacy and Intervention

In working with Martha in this study, I found myself emphasizing the importance of understanding the high school environment as fully as possible from the perspectives of the various participants (Mexican students and their parents, teachers, principal, superintendent, non-Mexican students). This was a continuing frustration for Martha, who wanted to move from understanding to intervention. About two thirds of the way through the first year of our research, I had a conference with Martha and her coadvisor, an African American male in his early 50s, regarding a paper Martha had written for his class. In her paper, she identified the forms of segregation she believed were being perpetrated against the Mexican students in the high school and argued for the formation of a tutoring program at the high school, sponsored by Latino/Latina graduate students from the University of Illinois. Her coadvisor cautioned Martha about the likelihood that shifting from understanding to intervention would result in our being asked to leave the school because of potential threats associated with the presence of outsiders, particularly university-based individuals. Martha objected strongly to his advice, and in frustration he exhorted her: "Martha, I've been Black lots longer than you've been Mexican!" By the end of our meeting, Martha had become convinced that he and I were status-quo academics—in fact, she accused both of us of advising her to "sell out."

Her comment bothered me a great deal because I had, over the years, come to view myself as an advocate for students who were marginalized by the educational system. In the many years I worked in elementary and secondary schools before becoming a university professor, I participated in conceptualizing and implementing educational policies and programs specifically designed to provide individuals of all ages with choices they would not otherwise have had. I like to believe that my university teaching and research interests continue to reflect a focus on improved access and conditions of learning for students historically marginalized in mainstream educational settings. Martha's accusation, however, led me to question the extent to which my commitment to these goals was consistent with the manner in which I had conceptualized the study at Agriville Junior/Senior High School.

Disillusionment With the School's Resistance to Change

The second year of our study witnessed the appointment of a new principal and counselor, both of whom were much more student-centered in general as well as more sensitive to the needs of the Mexican students in particular than were their predecessors; but there was no appreciable change in the ways in which the schooling experiences of the limited- and non-English-speaking students had improved. This was extremely frustrating for both Martha and me, particularly since in the fall of that second year there were signs of activism among a few Mexican parents and high school teachers who were determined that the year would reflect genuine improvements in the conditions of teaching and learning for the Mexican immigrants in the school.

The fact that there was so little change from the first to the second year of our study provided support for Martha's position that positive change was virtually impossible because the optimal time for modifying school practices and policies to accommodate the newly arrived immigrants was the initial year, when the administrators, teachers, and Mexican students were first becoming acquainted with each other. Martha believed that the critical moment for change had passed and that in the second year of our study, administrators, teachers, students and parents had settled into routines and attitudes that alienated each from the other; most importantly, the Mexican immigrants and their families had come to view school as a "holding place" that had no relevancy to them.

Martha had, by the second year, effectively given up direct participation in the study. She felt unable to continue documenting the failure of the Mexican students without being able to provide the kinds of intervention she believed would have been effective in improving the social and academic success of these students. She was discouraged by the intractability of the school and its resistance to change, and she was further disappointed by the lack of achievement motivation displayed by a number of the Mexican students she had attempted to tutor.

MY RESPONSE TO THE ISSUES EMERGING FROM MY COLLABORATION WITH MARTHA

Although I care very deeply about improving the educational and social experiences of the Mexican immigrants in Agriville High School, I am also very much aware of the complexity of the change process, the difficulties associated with identifying what needs to be changed, and how and by whom, as well as the length of time for changes to become institutionalized in schools. As I talk with Martha about her passion for intervention, I agree with her that the first year of our study was an important year and that a number of changes could have been implemented that might have improved the newly arrived immigrants' chances for social and academic success in the high school. Although Martha and I could have, in that first year, identified a number of specific changes that might have improved learning conditions for the Mexican students, I do not think that either of us at that point understood enough about the school, the students, and their families to specify correctly how these changes could best be made or by whom they should have been made.

For example, as stated earlier, Martha and I had no difficulties in identifying the "victims" of the high school system in the first few weeks we were there. We were also fairly convinced about construing specific teachers as the "villains." Not until we were well into the second half of our study did Martha's and my continued association with the teachers and students reveal the complex nature of the interactions occurring among the administrators, teachers, students, and their parents. The information gained from the additional time spent in understanding these interactions yielded the observation that, for the most part, teachers and administrators who were well intentioned but poorly informed, rather than truly bigoted, accounted for the majority of the problematic educational policies and practices encountered by the Mexican students and their families. This is not to say, however, that Martha and I did not identify teachers whose interactions with the Mexican students appeared to be conditioned by negative ethnic stereotypes, although we came to believe that such teachers were few in number. The second year of the study afforded Martha and me the opportunity to develop a deeper level of understanding, from which we were able to move more confidently toward advocacy and intervention.

Despite the fact that Martha and I began our study with a commitment to developing an understanding of the interactions between rural, White, high school educators and newly arrived, limited- and non-English speaking Mexican immigrants, it is important to acknowledge that our very presence in the high school was a form of intervention. For example, the fact that our study focused on newly arrived Mexican immigrants signaled our interest in this group and made teachers more aware of their interactions with these students than might otherwise have been the case, at least during the times Martha and I were in the school.

Martha's presence had a huge impact on the Mexican and non-Mexican students as well as on the principal and teachers, none of whom had ever known a Mexican American woman who was pursuing a doctoral degree. I collected and shared with teachers names of companies that published high school textbooks in Spanish, and I provided the Spanish teacher with information about external sources of funding for programs that could provide classroom teachers with the kinds of additional resources they needed to work effectively with the Mexican students. Evidence of our influence was also reflected by the fact that Martha and I were invited by one of the local factory owners to advise him on the kinds of resources he and other local employers should provide to the school in order for the administrators and teachers to educate the children of their Mexican employees more effectively.

This invitation, and Martha's and my response to it, highlighted the fundamental issues with which she and I struggled as we conducted research in the school. The invitation provided us with a tangible means of reconciling differing views of the research act, that is, understanding versus advocacy and intervention. Our 2 years of involvement in the school increased our understanding of the interactions between the high school teachers and the newly arrived, limited- and non-English-speaking Mexican students in their classrooms. I believed that the level of understanding Martha and I achieved during our study was sufficient for us to collaborate with educators and community members as they contemplated various interventions for improving the education of the Mexican students in the school. Thus, when presented with the opportunity to collaborate on related school improvement initiatives, I responded with enthusiasm; I felt I had reached my initial research goal of understanding, and I was ready to participate in designing a community-based intervention program. What I was not ready for was Martha's unwillingness to participate in the endeavor.

Martha rejected the invitation for a number of reasons, including her commitment to completing the doctoral degree in a timely manner and her fear that time spent on other projects would interfere with completion of this degree. Martha was also concerned that she would be blamed for the failure of any intervention with which she was associated, and that her failure would validate the perceptions of those who like to claim that even highly educated Mexican Americans are incapable of "helping their own." Martha's response to the invitation surprised her and provoked a serious identity crisis; her decision not to collaborate with community members appeared to contradict her stated commitment to advocacy and intervention and suggested the possibility that she had acquiesced to a perception of researchers as detached from the people they seek to understand. The seeming contradictions both alarmed and discouraged her. I realized that Martha's response resulted, in part, from my inability to address satisfactorily the concerns regarding race and ethnicity, subjectivity, positionality, and view of research that she had raised throughout our study in Agriville; this admission frustrated and saddened me.

Martha's experiences in Agriville made her question whether or not she wanted to pursue an academic career, if being a researcher meant that what one did was observe rather than participate in improving situations. As a means of addressing these and other issues that emerged from our research together, we began exploring alternative research models that challenged traditional approaches to scholarship. Despite her concerns about the profession, in the 3 years following the Agriville study, Martha completed her PhD studies and accepted a post doctoral fellowship in a large research university.

Reflections

I have spent the majority of my career working with students who are significantly out of synch with the mainstream model of schooling. My decision to focus my efforts on this kind of student is directly related to the marginalization I myself experienced as a result of being labeled as culturally deprived and economically disadvantaged within the dominant school culture. These schooling experiences shaped both my teaching and research goals; and in the course of pursuing these, I have frequently worked with students of color whose families are poor. On such occasions, my race most clearly differentiates me from them; although race has played a powerful role in conditioning my lived experiences, it is insufficient for understanding who I am and how I think.

Many of the issues with which I struggled while conducting the study in Agriville have been discussed by other researchers who have looked deeply and critically at issues of subjectivity and positionality, and have raised serious challenges to the methodology as well as the purpose of research. The notion that individuals are constructed of multiple, often hyphenated, identities has been discussed by a number of researchers (e.g., Dickar,1997; Estrada & McLaren, 1993; Fine, 1994; Foster, 1994; Trinh, 1990; Peshkin, 1988; Scheurich, 1993). Although the concept of multiple identities is useful in illustrating the complexities involved in representing oneself to others, this cannot compensate for the fact that labels of any kind impose restrictions on a person's identity. That is, regardless of the categorical labels that we use to describe ourselves, these labels remain necessary but insufficient for understanding who we are (Stanfield & Dennis, 1993).

In our society, race or ethnicity is often used as a simple proxy for "making sense" of people—a way of reducing the complexity of identity for the purposes of accepting or rejecting them. Racial and ethnic identities as socially constructed have persisted as powerful sorting mechanisms in our society and have been resistant to redefinition at a national, much less an individual level. Although the social construction of race continues to systematically privilege White persons and repeatedly penalize other people of color, there are serious problems associated with conceptualizing identity as a set of dichotomous categories

Despite the highly differentiated rewards and sanctions linked to various racial and ethnic identities, and the intractability of these categories, I envision individuals' multiple identities as generally more fluid than static, with some identities becoming more or less salient at different times, changing in response to conditions that are internal as well as external to the individual. I believe that the way in which various identities intersect and influence interactions with others is determined partly by the individuals themselves, partly by the people with whom they interact and partly by the conditions under which they have come together. Much like different-colored shards of glass in a kaleidoscope, these identities can merge to create a wide variety of images that are temporal in nature and reflective of the particular positionalities we occupy at any given moment.

The majority of my interactions with Agriville staff were conditioned by perceptions of shared identities that were revealed as the year progressed. I believe that several of these identities were of particular importance to my gaining access to the principal and teachers, and I would prioritize them as my being: (a) White; (b) a former classroom teacher; (c) a product of a small rural town; (d) middle aged. In thinking about my interactions with the Mexican students, I believe that they tolerated my presence because they first identified Martha as "one of them," and Martha, in turn, identified me as her teacher and her friend. Although I had a number of characteristics in common with the Agriville staff, I do not feel that I "over-identified" with them or became an advocate for their actions. With respect to the Mexican students, however, I believe that I tended to do just that, perhaps in an attempt to minimize the very real differences between us, perhaps out of a falsely held (but cherished) belief that they and I had something in common—that I "understood" their "oppression"—when in fact, I could not.

The tendency for White researchers to do such things—to co-opt the other's experience—has been criticized by a number of researchers (e.g., Anzaldua, 1990; Delgado, 1995; Dickar, 1997; Fine, 1994; Scheurich, 1993; Sleeter, 1993; Stanfield & Dennis, 1993; Tate, 1997; Villenas, 1996). Familiarity with this literature was necessary, but not sufficient, for adequately monitoring my own subjectivities during the research process. Furthermore, the substantial amount of work that I have done with Native American educators, which, by agreement, is directed by their needs, goals, and preferences and is situated within their cultural context, was not enough to prevent me from lapsing into culturally biased patterns of research. I did not transfer the lessons that I had learned from my Native American colleagues to the Agriville study, although these lessons could have informed that research process usefully.

In some ways, my relative inattention to these issues during the Agriville study was a bit like my listening to meditation tapes while plunging into holiday traffic, hurling criticisms at my fellow drivers but ignoring my own driving errors as well as the messages of peace and compassion emanating from the tapes. In the end, what catapulted me into critiquing my own "taken-for-granted" behavior during the research process was Martha's unhappiness over the way things were going and her willingness to be straightforward in sharing her concerns with me. This, in turn, led to my revisiting the literature on critical theory and to my engaging in a deeper critique (with myself and others) of my motivations and actions with respect to the people I am seeking to understand.

With respect to Martha's and my differing views of the research process, I tended to focus my efforts on describing what was occurring between the Mexican students and their teachers in order to understand better how these interactions contributed to the Mexican students' academic and social difficulties in the school. When Martha felt that she sufficiently understood what was happening in the school, however, she felt it was time to direct her energies toward designing and implementing intervention strategies that would improve the academic achievement and attainment of the Mexican students.

Martha's commitment to action was rooted in her belief that many of the educational and social needs of the Mexican students required immediate attention, and that these needs could not be deferred for a period of months while we conducted our classroom observations and interviews. Martha perceived the teachers as unresponsive to the students and intent on maintaining the existing hierarchical structure and power distribution of the community (Apple, 1997; Foster, 1994) which subordinated the Mexican families in the area. As a consequence, her aim was to create a tutorial program for the Mexican students, staffed by graduate students from the university and located outside of the Agriville school system. Unlike Martha, the mark I was trying to hit was that of description and understanding so that the findings of the Agriville study could be used to inform policy and practice regarding the education of limited- and non-English-speaking teenage immigrants in Agriville and elsewhere.

Critical theorists (e.g., Anzaldua, 1987; Apple, 1997; Collins, 1991; Delgado-Gaitan, 1993; Fine, 1994; Foster, 1994 ; Lather, 1991; Scheurich, 1993; Sleeter, 1993; Stanfield, 1992), advocate research that moves from description and understanding to emancipatory action in collaboration with those who have been subjected to the domination of others. Although at times, Martha and I appeared to have missed the mark with one another regarding our views of the research process in Agriville, I believe we were actually occupying different points along the continuum, from understanding to action.

Our divergent and sometimes oppossional perspectives and actions were related in part to our differing racial and ethnic identities, subjectivities, positionalities, and views of the research process. It was, however, the friendship and trust that had developed between us over the years that eventually made it possible for us to begin to examine the nature and consequences of our interactions with one another, and to explore the ways in which these interactions shaped the research process in which we engaged. This was by no means an easy process, nor has it been concluded as such. Martha and I continue to examine why and where we target our energies as educational researchers and where we hit or miss the mark with each other when working together for the purposes of understanding and transformation.

My experiences working with Martha in Agriville have disrupted my comfort level and challenged my relative inattention to the privileges associated with my race and position. Paradoxically, my experiences have also highlighted the inadequacies of various labels and categorical schemes. Whether they are constructed to legitimate or to oppose existing power arrangements, these labels promise more information than they can deliver and are insufficient for representing the complexity and the contradictions embedded in myself and others. Although I believe that it is essential to continue examining the ways in which my race and ethnicity, subjectivities, positionalities, and views of research shape not only my motives but my actions, I am convinced that self-reflection is not enough. With respect to the Agriville study, I needed Martha to critique my motives and actions in ways that I had not been able or willing to do until she risked talking with me about her concerns regarding the design and purpose of the study. I believe that collaborative research holds much promise, if carried out in an atmosphere of openness, respect, and perhaps most importantly, compassion. Talk of compassion is notably absent from the literature, although Scheurich (1993) acknowledges its absence in his own work and argues for its use. When I speak about the need for compassion in research, I refer to compassion for self as well as others—a compassion that moves beyond blame—a space in which harmony and dissonance can coexist in ways that challenge and extend the boundaries of our understanding, so that we and those who participate in the research process with us not only transform the situations in which we find ourselves, but also are transformed by our interactions with each other.

REFERENCES

Anzaldua, G. (1987). *Borderlands/La frontera*. San Francisco: Aunt Lute Books.

Anzaldua, G. (1990). *Making face, making soul (haciendo caras): Creative and critical perspectives by women of color*. San Francisco: Aunt Lute Foundation Books.

Apple, M. W. (Ed.). (1997). *Review of research in education*. Washington, DC: American Educational Research Association.

Collins, P. H. (1991). *Black feminist thought: Knowledge, consciousness, and the politics of empowerment*. New York: Routledge.

Delgado, R. (1995). The imperial scholar revisited: How to marginalize outsider writing, ten years later. In R. Delagado (Ed.), *Critical race theory: The cutting edge* (pp. 401–408). Philadelphia: Temple University Press.

Delgado-Gaitan, C. (1993). Researching change and changing the researcher. *Harvard Educational Review, 63*, 389–411.

Dickar, M. (1997). Teaching in our underwear: The liabilities of whiteness in the racial classroom. *Researcher, 11* (2), 17–23.

Estrada, K. & McLaren, P. (1993). A dialogue on multiculturalism and democratic culture. *Educational Researcher, 22* (3), 27–33.

Fine, M. (1994). Working the hyphens: Reinventing self and other in qualitative research. In N. Denzin & Y. Lincoln (Eds.), *Handbook of qualitative research* (pp. 70–82). Thousand Oaks, CA: Sage.

Foster, M. (1994). The power to know one thing is never the power to know all things: Methodological notes on two studies of Black American teachers. In A. Gitlin (Ed.), *Power and Method: Political activism and educational research* (pp. 129–146). New York: Routledge.

Lather, P. (1991). *Getting smart: Feminist research and pedagogy with/in the postmodern*. New York: Routledge.

Trinh T. (1990). Not you/like you: Post-colonial women an the interlocking questions of identity and difference. In G. Anzaldua (Ed.), *Making face, making soul: Creative and critical perspectives of feminists of color (pp 371–373)*. San Francisco, CA: Aunt Lute Books.

Peshkin, A. (1988). In search of subjectivity—one's own. *Educational Researcher, 17* (7), 17–22.

Scheurich, J. J. (1993). Toward a White discourse on racism. *Educational Researcher, 22* (8), 5–10.

Sleeter, C. E. (1993). Advancing a White discourse: A response to Scheurich. *Educational Researcher, 22* (8), 13–15.

Stanfield, J. H. II, & Dennis, R. M. (Eds.). (1993). *Race and ethnicity in research methods*. Newbury Park, CA: Sage.

Tate, W. F. IV, (1997). Critical race theory and education: History, theory, and implications. In M. W. Apple (Ed.), *Review of research in education* (pp. 195–247). Washington, DC: American Educational Research Association.

2

*La mojada y el coyote:** Experiences of a Wetback Researcher

Martha Zurita
University of Minnesota, Twin Cities

As a graduate student, I learned the "proper ways" of conducting research and was socialized to the importance of researcher objectivity. The teaching styles and curriculum utilized in many of my methodology courses led me to believe that research was very much like doing mathematics; that is, if I followed a particular sequence of steps, I would be rewarded with the right answer. The formula involved selecting a topic, picking a site, identifying a sample, collecting and analyzing the data, and writing up the findings. Rarely was there any discussion in these classes of the ways in which a researcher's gender and/or race and ethnicity mediated these steps. Fortunately, I now realize that many of the notions I was taught early in my graduate career have been vigorously critiqued by a number of scholars. Many feminist researchers (Fine, 1994; Lather, 1994; Patai, 1994; Warren, 1988) and researchers of color (Foster, 1994; Rosaldo, 1989; Stanfield, 1993a, 1993b, 1994; Villenas, 1996) have introduced alternative research methodologies that have created spaces for researchers whose backgrounds and perspectives differ from those who have historically dominated the field of educational research.

Issues that have been raised by this literature include the reporting of information (Fine, 1994); the relationship between researcher and researched

---

*The idea for this title (La mojada y el coyote) came from Villenas (1996).

(Foster, 1994; Stanfield, 1993a; Villenas, 1996); calls to social action through research (Fine, 1994; Gitlin, 1994); insider/outsider positionality (Foster, 1994; LeCompte & McLaughlin, 1994); and ethics in researching people of color and other oppressed groups (Stanfield, 1993b). The majority of this literature focuses on the relationships between the researcher, the researched, and the world of academe, such as researcher ethics. This chapter, however, examines the relationships between the researcher and the gatekeepers who facilitate or hinder the researcher's access to research participants (Zurita, 1997). Specifically, this chapter examines the relationship between me, the gatekeepers in a midwestern high school (teachers, administrators, staff), and the Mexican students I was attempting to study. In relating my experiences with these gatekeepers, I hope to illustrate some of the ways in which a researcher's race or ethnicity can shape the nature and quality of the research he or she is attempting to conduct, particularly when this research involves studying issues related to members of the researcher's own racial or ethnic group in an oppressive situation (Foster, 1994; Stanfield, 1993a).

Although there were other factors, such as my relatively young age and graduate-student status that played roles in shaping my research experiences in the high school setting, I assert that my Mexican descent was the most powerful influence of all. In describing these experiences, I have organized the chapter in two major sections. The first section focuses on how the teachers and Mexican students viewed my presence in the high school. The second section examines issues I dealt with personally as a researcher of color in that setting.

THE SETTING

The events I describe in this chapter occurred in conjunction with my position as a research assistant working with Dr. Betty Merchant, who was conducting a study of a junior/senior high school in the rural Midwest. Approximately 91% of the students in this school were White, whereas 8% of the student body was Mexican. All of the teachers, administrators, and staff in the school were White. The only exception was one teacher who had a White father and a Mexican mother. This teacher was, however, considered White by all her colleagues in the school. The purpose of Dr. Merchant's study was to examine the socialization process of newly arrived, limited- and non-English-speaking Mexican immigrant students. There had been a large influx of this group of students because one of the two major factories in town had more than doubled in physical size and had recruited additional employees from Mexico over the summer to fill the new vacancies. Our study lasted 2 years and involved weekly all-day visits that consisted of interviews, tutoring sessions, and classroom observations.

The demographics of the town were similar to that of the school. Although the actual number of Mexicans residing in the town had not been clearly identified by local census takers, it was estimated that of the 3,000 residents, approximately 250 were Mexican. A very small number of the town's residents were Asian and Asian Indian. For the most part, the Mexican and White communities in the town did not intermingle. The majority of the Mexican residents lived in predominantly Mexican neighborhoods, one of which was located behind a major factory in town and the other in a trailer park near the freeway. Most of the Mexicans spoke Spanish predominantly, whereas the Whites spoke English.

PERSONAL BACKGROUND

I offer the following personal information in order to help the reader visualize what the teachers, staff, and students saw when they looked at me (Patai, 1994). In studying this group of students, I found myself to look very much like them. When we first began work on this study, I was 23 years old, yet I was told that I looked much younger. My professor reported that the first day we walked into the school, people thought she was my mother and that she was enrolling me in high school. With the exception of a few student teachers, I was the youngest nonstudent at the school and I looked even younger than many of the students.

I am a first-generation American, born to Mexican parents. I was born and raised on the west side of the city of Chicago. In the mid-1960s, my parents emigrated to the United States from the mountains of Durango, Mexico, with my three oldest siblings. My parents had a third grade education, and after coming to this country they were employed in factories. My father was a factory worker until his death in 1977. My mother still works in a factory.

I am the sixth of seven children and the second to attend and graduate from college. My brothers and sister who did not attend a university attended either a training school or a community college without receiving degrees. The title of "the first Zurita PhD" is proudly mine, although I am not treated any differently by my family members.

When identifying myself, I state that I am "Mexican," as do most Illinoisans of Mexican descent. I do so because the Mexican culture is so very near and dear to my heart, and I was raised in a Mexican home in American society. As such, I am fluent in speaking, writing, and reading both Spanish and English.

I am a person of color; the hue of my skin is a light brown. My paternal grandmother was a full-blooded Tarumaro Indian and her rich brown complexion was inherited by my brother and me, so when people look at me, they can see that I am "different." Although some notice my complexion, others notice my "accent." It is this difference, or my being Mexican, visibly Mexican, that has affected my research experiences so heavily. Furthermore, my being relatively young, my having Mexican, uneducated, factory-working, immigrant parents, and my being "Mexican" in identity and culture, all had a significant impact on my eventual connection to the Mexican students who were enrolled in the school in which I was working as a research assistant.

Professor Relations: El Coyote

My professor, Betty Merchant, and I differed greatly in several ways. She was visibly White, culturally American, in her late 40s, from a small northeastern town, an assistant professor, and non-Spanish speaking. Although we were very different, we had a very close working and personal relationship. We met 3 years earlier, while I was still an undergraduate; she was my mentor for 2 consecutive summers as part of the Summer Research Opportunities Program (SROP). After our involvement in the program, we maintained a working relationship, which quickly became a friendship. Betty, the first professor I knew on a first name basis, was instrumental in my decision to pursue a graduate degree and choose a life in academe.

Although Betty treated me as a respected colleague rather than as a student, the gatekeepers at the school did not view me in a similar fashion. In fact, the differential treatment Betty and I received from teachers and administrators forced us to reassess our relationship. After much thought, I came up with a perfect description of our relationship as stated by E. G. Murrillo, Jr.; "Like a 'mojado' [wetback] ethnographer, I attempt to cross the artificial borders into occupied academic territories, searching for a 'coyote' [smuggler] to secure a safe passage" (as quoted in Villenas, 1996, p. 711). I was treated as the mojada, whereas Betty was viewed as the coyote. I needed her to smuggle me across the border. Many times, it felt as though she was my sponsor in a foreign country. She held my green card, or validation into the country of research. The gatekeepers insisted that Betty keep the little Mexican girl under control and make sure that she did not stir up things.

From the beginning, Betty and I fell into very different roles. Because I was the only one who spoke Spanish, it was my responsibility to interact with the Mexican students who spoke limited or no English. After some time at the school, even the Mexican students who spoke English interacted mostly with me, rather than with Betty. On the other side of the coin, although we were both fluent in the English language, teachers talked almost exclusively with Betty during the first year of our study. Toward the end of our second year at the school, teachers talked with me, but usually on a superficial level or to seek assistance with Mexican students.

I approached Betty with my concerns about the differential treatment I was receiving from the teachers, in particular, and she did her best to help me in my interactions with them. She pointed out that female researchers face many of the same issues that I was facing, such as being pegged as unobjective by some and untrustworthy by others. Being both a woman and Mexican, I knew I was not facing these issues simply because I was a woman—it was due to my ethnicity. Betty could not really help me through these experiences because she was unable to truly understand what I was experiencing as a Mexican (Andersen, 1993). She did not even know where to begin to help me with the issues that were overwhelming me. One bit of advice she offered proved to be very therapeutic and resulted in this chapter. That was to keep a journal of my interactions at the school, as well as my reactions to and reflections about these interactions.

Experiences with Teachers: *La Migra* (The I.N.S.)

During visits to the school, I felt I was being treated differently than Betty by teachers and students. In fact, my treatment by the gatekeepers (i.e., teachers, administrators, and staff) was even different from that experienced by other Chicana researchers in similar settings. One example is that described by Villenas (1996) when she was researching Latino populations in North Carolina, a situation where she was largely accepted by the White gatekeepers. She was constantly used as an expert on the "Mexican problem" and as such, found herself privy to the beliefs of White gatekeepers, not only about the Latinos she was studying, but about Latinos in general. As she stated; "In more ways than one, I found it easier to be an insider to the community of dominant English-speaking leaders than to the Latino community" (Villenas, 1996, p. 724). In my case, I was hardly given this opportunity. From my first day at the school, I was treated as one of "them" by the "dominant English-speaking leaders." The treatment I experienced at the hands of the gatekeepers was, in my opinion, consistent with Warren's (1988) conclusion that "role taking in fieldwork is subsumed by a more interactive process in which respondents assign the fieldworker to what they see as his or her proper place in the social order" (p. 19). Similarly, Stanfield (1994) stated: "Even in 1990s terms, there is still a great deal of Eurocentric anxiety displayed toward well-educated people of color who 'act' too ethnic and, more than that, too independent" (p.172).

The almost linear progression of my treatment by teachers was as follows: (a) the "other;" (b) a tutor and hired hand; (c) "Mexican expert" and problem solver; and (d) a radical militant. In my first few weeks at the school, teachers appeared to be walking on eggshells around me. It appeared they had a "we–they" mentality. The Whites were the "we," because this was "their country"; and the Mexicans were the "they," because they invaded it. Due to my ethnicity, I was automatically put on the "they" team. I was treated as the "other" and it gave me the feeling that the two groups, Mexicans and Whites, were in opposition to each other or at war with each other and that the teachers feared I would automatically side with the Mexican students on any and every issue. They were clearly being extremely careful around me. This was apparent in their use of language, often pausing and mulling it over before saying "English students" and "Spanish students," as opposed to White and Mexican students, respectively. It was not only apparent in their choice of words, but also in the way they looked at me. While talking with my professor and me, many teachers would have apologetic looks on their faces whenever they made eye contact with me. The looks were very similar to the way one looks at a homeless puppy. It appeared as if they were being apologetic for not being able to teach the Mexican students and/or as if they were looking to me for justification that they were good, nonracist people who were trying their best. When both my professor and I were in the teachers' lounge, almost all of the teachers would solicit only my professor's opinions. This was especially true when it came to issues that appeared to be "sensitive" for me, such as multicultural education and bilingual education. I was only brought into discussions when trivial issues were being examined. When in the teachers' lounge without my professor, most teachers did not acknowledge my presence—not even with a "hello."

After gaining some trust among the teachers, I next felt I was being treated as a hired hand. Due to the fact that Mexican students constantly requested my assistance with homework and tests, teachers began to take my volunteer tutoring services for granted. They would send me students without asking if this were all right with me. Many of the times, teachers sent students to find me without even knowing if I was actually in the building. A few times, elementary teachers who did not know who I was would send me their students to be tutored. Other times, teachers would ask me to come into their classrooms and "evaluate the Mexican situations" (unofficially, of course) and give some "home remedies," despite the fact that my suggestions were seldom, if ever, taken seriously by them. At times, it felt as though I was simply being tested. It was perhaps during this stage that I grew to despise going to the school. I finally realized it was because I was (a) being overworked by doing literally two jobs: research assistant, and teachers' aide and personal assistant, at the same time doing the job that the teachers were not doing and could not do, and not receiving any sort of compensation and support; (b) being taken for granted by the teachers; and (c) being placed in an inferior position (i.e., teachers' aide) by the teachers. As a result of all these things, my role as a researcher in the school was negated.

After my first semester at the school, a small number of teachers, as well as the principal, began to approach me on a one-on-one basis, to ask indirectly for my assistance with Mexican students. Several times they would "casually" bring up minor student problems, such as misbehaving, eating in class, and tardiness, and then look to me for answers. I simply wanted to scream; "They do it because they're adolescents— that's their job, to annoy you." Because they linked these incidents with Mexican students only as the deviants, and raised the issues with me, as opposed to someone, anyone, else, I believe that these professionals actually thought that these students' deviance was a result of their ethnicity. Furthermore, because I was of the same ethnicity as these students, the teachers and principals often acted as if they believed I had some natural insight into what makes Mexican students eat in class or misbehave. In my opinion, they had labeled me a "Mexican expert"; yet the one time that I decided to play this role, it did no good. At the start of our second year in the school, the new principal came to me one day and asked my opinion about two eighth grade girls who had been misbehaving all of the last year I had observed them. He wanted to know what to do about them. My response was short and simple: "Call their parents." No Mexican child wants his/her parents to miss work and lose an hour or two of pay, especially to experience embarrassment over the child's disrespect. The principal dismissed my recommendation and mumbled that he would use it as a final step. So why ask my opinion? His reaction made me question this whole "Mexican expert" role and how seriously my opinions were taken by the teachers and the principals. Did they tell me of the misbehavior of the Mexican students because they wanted me to give them suggestions on how to deal with the behavior? Did they want me to handle the situations for them by using my friendships with these students? Were they trying to make me aware of the fact that the very students I wanted to help were not saints, but deviants? Or did they want me to feel part of the blame and shame for the students' wrongdoings, due to our shared ethnicity and friendship? On reflection, I can honestly say that I would answer Yes to all of these questions.

In the final stages of the first school year, some teachers expressed concerns that I had prepped students to shout "Discrimination!" and "Racism!" at teachers, and had encouraged the students to engage in defiant actions at school. These accusations could not have been farther from the truth. First of all, it appeared that the originators of these accusations were two teachers who should have had closer ties to the Mexican communities, namely the ESL teacher and the half-Mexican Spanish teacher. In reflecting on the situation, I believe that the motivation for these allegations was jealousy on their part. These teachers were extraordinarily wary of me from the very beginning. As time went by, I gained popularity with the Mexican students while their popularity levels decreased. Secondly, the students who were expressing these views were not under study. These students were American-born students of Mexican descent; as such, I did not have contact with them, other than a casual "hello." The teachers, however, did not examine this very important fact and continued to blame me for these students' views.

This occurrence raised two interesting points. First, the students were making very powerful and potentially explosive accusations that their teachers were discriminating against them. Yet the teachers dismissed those accusations and blamed me rather than examining the internal structure of the school, the town, and, more importantly, themselves. It was easier to "blame the Mexican," which is another phrase I coined during my research experiences in this school. The second point deals with something my mother taught me. She made it clear that people of color have to go far and beyond what Whites do in order to be considered equally capable. This was my first time out on the field. Although I tried to blend in as researchers were supposed to, the teachers at the high school were watching my every step, listening to my every word. They continued to view me as an outsider and intruder. The more time I spent in the school, the more popular I became with the Mexican students. This occurred as some teachers were becoming increasingly unpopular with these students. This made me more susceptible to scrutiny. When people who from the beginning do not trust or like you set out to analyze you, chances are they will find something against you, regardless of whether it is true or not (i.e., the militant claims). As a result, I learned I had to run a tighter ship, as my mother warned. This final stage of treatment by teachers put a damper on my enthusiasm for research and made me extremely cautious around students, especially when teachers were around.

Experiences with Students: One of "Them"

Although my experiences with the teachers dampened my enthusiasm for research, the relationships I developed with the Mexican students helped me realize the importance of my presence (Foster, 1994). It was this that motivated me to continue as a researcher. The roles that the Mexican students attributed to me were as follows: (a) a teacher; (b) a tutor; (c) a problem solver and advocate; and (d) a friend.

When I first arrived at the school, the students were confused as to my position. They continually referred to me as *maestra* (teacher) and would frequently raise their hands while talking to me in small groups. During my first few weeks in the school, the Mexican students would stare at me strangely in the hallways and keep their distance as if testing the waters. When we interviewed or talked with these students, it appeared that we were embarrassing them; if their friends walked by, they would not look at or speak to each other. It was almost as if they were being punished by our talking to them. They would answer interview questions very carefully, and sometimes untruthfully. The truth would come out during later interviews or tutoring sessions. They would also use language that was proper (i.e., not language used with friends).

After a few months, students began to request my tutoring services quite often, and they began to treat me in a less formal manner. They came to see me more as a tutor than a teacher. An interesting change was that the students were no longer embarrassed when I was with them. I had become a rare commodity; I had something they needed (content knowledge and language proficiency) and was willing to give it to them. A major problem was that there was only one of me and more than fifteen of them. Every time I would pass the study hall or an open door, I would hear "Pssst, pssst" or "*Marta, no me ayudas?*" (Martha, won't you help me?) They also began to address me by name, instead of using the formal title of *maestra*. It was around this time that students began to answer my questions more quickly, without the pondering, and more truthfully, in that they revealed disillusions and dissatisfactions with the school and town that they had not shared with me earlier. More things were revealed during tutoring sessions. It became clear that many of these students, especially those who came directly from Mexico as opposed to those who came from Texas, were advanced in content knowledge. When I would explain many of the subjects in Spanish, especially mathematics, they knew exactly what I was referring to and had their own names for procedures; it was simply that they did not understand what the teacher was saying in English. Although they knew the content, they were not learning the importance of study skills and phonetics. When they visited the ESL teacher, she would simply give them the answers to their assignments because she was overloaded with students. The students came to expect the same of me, and although they were initially upset, they were eventually happy when I turned our tutoring sessions into lectures and group work sessions. My role as tutor continued through the 2 years of fieldwork in the school. In fact, one student came to visit the university campus in the spring of our second year, and the first thing he reported was that the other students were requesting that I return to the school to assist them with their exams.

Along with requests for assistance with their course work came student requests for help in solving problems with teachers and in advocating for them on such matters as book collections and fees. The requests were partly due to the fact that the ESL teacher was located in the elementary school, and as a result was not readily available to the Mexican students to assist them in emergencies that would arise. Another reason for these requests might have been the fact that I was not a teacher and unlike the ESL teacher had no tie to the school, and as a result was viewed by students as less likely to side automatically with the school. I was the youngest nonstudent there; perhaps this also helped them feel that I was not a threat and would not treat them condescendingly for losing a book or getting into a fight. The final, and I believe the most important, reason for the requests they made of me was the fact that I was Mexican, visibly Mexican. Everyone around them was White: teachers, staff, students. I was Mexican and had more power than they did, and because I helped them through tutoring they knew I would try and help them in other ways as well. They trusted me because we not only shared a language, but a culture and history (Foster, 1994).

During the final months of the school year, the students came to view me and treat me as a friend. During the "tutor" stage, the students' first response when they saw me was to flag me down and ask for help during their study hours. During the "friend" stage, female students would first hug me, and both male and female students would ask where I had been, why I had not returned earlier, and other questions of that nature. After inquiring about me as a person, they would then ask for help with homework. I felt as though I had truly gained their trust, respect, and friendship. They would discuss with me issues they were facing in classes, with teachers, and at home. I was invited to their homes, to hang out with them after school and during weekends, and even to their cotillions in Mexico during the winter break. When I graciously declined the invitations to the cotillions and stated that I did not have a means of transportation, I was offered rides with their families. Although they still needed me for academic reasons, I felt that our relationships had gone beyond tutor–tutee and researcher–researched. When I walked through the halls, three to five students walked with me chatting about themselves and their lives, not about algebra. It was at this stage that I felt we had received the *most* honest interviews during our time at the school.

PERSONAL DILEMMAS

In addition to not knowing exactly where I stood with the teachers and students, I faced many personal dilemmas as a result of being a researcher of color, which I describe in this section. These dilemmas revolved around something I had learned as an undergraduate. During that time, an African American professor made me aware of a belief that was prevalent in the research world that, as researchers of color, we could not research our own groups because we could not and would not be completely objective (Fine,

1994; Foster, 1994; Rosaldo, 1989; Stanfield, 1994). Throughout the study, this notion plagued me, consciously and subconsciously; it was magnified by the teachers' initial treatment of me. The situation in which I was working brought me face-to-face with the claim that researchers of color could not objectively study members of their same racial or ethnic group.

During our first visits, both Betty and I realized that most, if not all, of the Mexican students in the school would definitely fail; they did not know the language, and if they knew survival English, they did not have the study or reading skills necessary for academic success. As a result of my undergraduate training in mathematics and my fluency in Spanish, I was capable of helping these students when they requested my assistance. Realizing I was just one person, who could not simultaneously tutor everyone who needed assistance and do the interviews that were necessary to the study we were conducting, I thought about bringing Latino undergraduate students into the town on Saturdays and having the Mexican parents pay for their transportation. This way, each high school student would receive needed instruction for at least 3 hours a week. This illusion was quickly dispelled, however. I was immediately made aware of the fact that my intervention would compromise the purpose of the study, which was to view the students in their natural setting and to document what would normally happen in the school if I had not been there to assist the Mexican students.

At this point, I faced a personal dilemma: How could I just sit back and watch these students fail? How could I refuse the assistance they so needed and I could so easily provide, and yet still extract information from them? Was this the game of research—to take and not give back? (Fine, 1994; Stanfield, 1993a, 1993b, 1994). There was also a more personal twist: Knowing what my older brothers and sister experienced as newly arrived immigrants, how could I *knowingly* put these students through similar experiences? It was as if all of this, which was defined as research and was for the good of students to come, went against everything I stood for. Furthermore, and perhaps more troublesome to me, was the question: Was my willingness to assist these students *admitting* that those of color could not research their own? Was it fuel for the enemy, who was on the sidelines waiting for this Mexican graduate student to fail and illustrate that people of color could not make good, objective researchers? As paranoid as it may sound, these were very real concerns to me.

As much as my professor, Betty, tried, I knew that she could not mentor me on this issue. I was very careful who I talked to about my concerns. I worried that if I voiced these concerns to unsympathetic ears, our research would be labeled invalid. As a result, I raised the issues with my advisor, an African American male in his 50s. He told me that I should intervene in the students' lives as little as possible—I could tutor, but should not attempt to implement an intervention program (Foster, 1994). Our meeting bothered me and left me feeling incomplete because he had not answered the bulk of my questions. In fact, he had left me with more questions than I had started with. This man, who appeared to understand what I was telling him based on his personal and research experiences, could easily tell me to let go of my attempt to help these students. Until this time, I had always felt that we had a bond; he knew what it was like being a rarity; he had been a graduate student when there were very few African American graduate students, and this was similar to my being a Mexican graduate student when there are not many Mexican graduate students in the Midwest. To my mind, he was basically saying, "Let the students fail." This meeting raised the final and perhaps the most profound dilemma I have been faced with as a result of this study. How can someone, especially a person of color, who reportedly became a professor to help students, advocate sitting back and watching them fail? Is this what academia does to you? Was this my future? And if I refused to give into this "me" thinking (as opposed to "they" thinking), did I have a future as a researcher? As stated earlier, I entered college with the hope of helping people and I believed that the more credentials I had, the more people would listen to me. Little did I realize the extent to which the educational system could change you without your even being aware of it (Foster, 1994).

This is a lesson I quickly learned. The second year of our study, a new principal was hired. He called on the community business leaders to provide financial assistance to the school for additional resources to improve the education of the Mexican students. Much to my surprise, they asked for me by name to work with my professor on implementing a program to help the Mexican students. When my professor informed me of their request, my response was a flat "No." No, I did not have the time to begin another project. No, I was trying to get my degree program completed by the following year. No, I did not want to be the scapegoat if the intervention program went bad—I did not want to give them the opportunity to "blame the Mexican" again. The bottom line was no. It then occurred to me that I had become much like the advisor from whom I had sought guidance. I went in wanting to create change, and when I was given the opportunity on a platter I refused it (Stanfield, 1994). This troubled me deeply because it had dawned on me that I had been changed by academia without realizing it (Foster, 1994). In order to deal with this dilemma, I conversed with a few Latino graduate students. One wise friend shared a profound phrase that put everything into perspective: "If you pretend to be something long enough, you become it."

PARTING THOUGHTS

Looking back at my experiences as a research assistant, and reviewing this chapter, I realize that I have learned a great deal. I have become aware of the fact that my role as a Mexican researcher is even more important than I had originally thought. Furthermore, I feel it is important to share my experiences with others like me, as well as those unlike me.

I have learned that gaining access and acceptability in a research context is not as simple as educational researchers and university professors make it appear. The process of conducting research is not the same for everyone, and this process is shaped, in part, by the researcher's race and ethnicity in ways that are only now being made explicit. Educational researchers can teach you how to take field notes and code and analyze data, but do they tell you how to deal with the interpersonal issues that result from the intersection of your research activities and your race or ethnicity? Oftentimes, professors and other researchers act as if the research site is a lab—straightforward and controlled. It may be that easy for some researchers, especially those who claim race does not matter. Those of us for whom it is a factor, however, have to fend for ourselves, despite our disillusionment when we realize things are not as clear-cut as we have been led to believe. Although there is no handbook to guide us in such matters, I am hopeful that this chapter illuminates some of the complexities of the research process that have been discounted or ignored for far too long.

REFERENCES

Andersen, M. L. (1993). Studying across difference: Race, class, and gender in qualitative research. In J. H. Stanfield II & R. M. Dennis (Eds.), *Race and ethnicity in research methods* (pp. 39–52). Newbury Park, CA: Sage.

Fine, M. (1994). Distance and other stances: Negotiations of power inside feminist research. In A. Gitlin (Ed.), *Power and method: Political activism and educational research* (pp. 13–35). New York: Routledge.

Foster, M. (1994). The power to know one thing is never the power to know all things: Methodological notes on two studies of Black American teachers. In A. Gitlin (Ed.), *Power and method: Political activism and educational research* (pp. 129–146). New York: Routledge.

Gitlin, A. (1994). The shifting terrain of methodological debates. In A. Gitlin (Ed.), *Power and method: Political activism and educational research*, pp. 1–12). New York: Routledge.

Lather, P. (1994). Fertile obsession: Validity after poststructuralism. In A. Gitlin (Ed.), *Power and method: Political activism and educational research* (pp. 36–60). New York: Routledge.

LeCompte, M. D. & McLaughlin, D. (1994). Witchcraft and blessings, science and rationality: Discourses of power and silence in collaborative work with Navajo schools. In A. Gitlin (Ed.), *Power and method: Political activism and educational research* (pp. 147–165). New York: Routledge.

Patai, D. (1994). When method becomes power (Response). In A. Gitlin (Ed.), *Power and method: Political activism and educational research* (pp. 61–73). New York: Routledge.

Rosaldo, R. (1989). *Culture and truth: The remaking of social analysis*. Boston: Beacon Press.

Stanfield, J. H. II. (1993a). Methodological reflections: An introduction. In J. H. Stanfield II & R. M. Dennis (Eds.), *Race and ethnicity in research methods* (pp. 3–15). Newbury Park, CA: Sage.

Stanfield, J. H. II. (1993b). Epistemological considerations. In J. H. Stanfield II & R. M. Dennis (Eds.), *Race and ethnicity in research methods* (pp. 16–36). Newbury Park, CA: Sage.

Stanfield, J. H. II. (1994). Empowering the culturally diversified sociological voice (Response). In A. Gitlin (Ed.), *Power and method: Political activism and educational research* (pp. 166–175). New York: Routledge.

Villenas, S. (1996). The colonizer/colonized Chicana ethnographer: Identity, marginalization, and co-optation in the field. *Harvard Educational Review, 66*(4), 711–731.

Warren, C. A. B. (1988). *Gender issues in field research.* Newbury Park, CA: Sage.

Zurita, M. (1997). *One of "them:" Experiences of a Chicana researching Mexicanos.* Paper presented at the American Educational Research Association Annual Meeting, New York, NY.

3

"You Should Know What's Right for Me!" A Hybrid's Struggle to Define Empowerment for Critical Feminist Research in Education*

Lubna Nazir Chaudhry
University of Georgia, Athens

I begin this chapter with a poem I wrote almost 5 years ago. It is a poem triggered off by actual incidents:

Something I want to share with all women

A woman in a *chaddar* looking through a microscope,
Struck a male white academic as incongruous,
He found the incongruity so amusing,
He put the picture on the wall,
"You know, ha, ha," he tells every visitor to his office,
"Here"s a perfect illustration of how education does not necessarily
entail consciousness."

*Adapted from a paper presented at the American Educational Research Association Meeting, San Francisco, 1995

A woman in a bikini ready to delve into the depths of the ocean,
Titillated the analytical mind of a brown male academic,
He found the scene augmented his ideas,
He put the picture on the wall,
"You can see the decadence of the Western Civilization here,"
He says about ten times a day, "All they can do is strip themselves."

Why us? I want to ask both of them.
Why us as exclusive representatives of the East and the West?
Why us when we represent what they both have in common?
Why us when it is they who make us wear *chaddars*, sell our bi-
kini-clad pictures?

WHY US?

When I wrote the poem in 1990, it was written as a celebration of universal sisterhood, that is, we women, in the East and the West, are all oppressed by patriarchies, through their representations, through their perceptions, and through their objectification. The questions evoked by this very poem at this juncture in my life are: What exactly is consciousness, and who defines it?

I am a self-identified Pakistani Muslim female in the United States, a cultural hybrid, engaged in critical feminist ethnographic analysis of the processes whereby self-identified Pakistani Muslim females forge hybrid cultural identities in response to their experiences and interaction with changing contextual realities within formal educational as well as community contexts. Using participant observation and interview–interactional data collection techniques, I was in the "field" for 2 years, April 1992 to April 1994. As a critical feminist researcher, I am very cognizant of the power imbalance in the researcher–researched relationship, and have attempted to mitigate the inequity through developing reciprocal relationships and offering my services as a broker in school and community contexts.

Furthermore, I conceived of this research project in itself as being empowering for the research participants. In order for feminist research to be nonexploitative, reciprocal, and praxis oriented, Lather (1991) suggests that the design should incorporate a component to measure the extent to which the study has empowered the participants. This "catalytic validity" should represent the degree to which the research has proved instrumental in energizing the participants to know reality in order to transform it—a process that requires the confrontation of false consciousness, and parallels Freire's (1970) concept of "conscientization." How exactly can such a conception be translated into meaningful practice in a research context where the feminist educational researcher is working with those for whom the *chaddar*, the Muslim veil, represents the ultimate consciousness? What constitutes empowerment and resistance for women whose realm of reality lies outside or at least on the margins of the discursive possibilities of feminism in its available forms? What implications does this problem of empowerment have for the role of the culturally hybrid feminist who is ambivalently situated vis-à-vis the *chaddar* as well as the Western, liberal, post-civil rights discourse of human rights, freedom of expression, and agency that characterizes much of feminist discourse?

My endeavor is to grapple with these questions through a critical synopsis of two episodes as represented in my field notes, as well as my analytical memory, not in a bid to provide any answers, but to highlight the complexity and significance of these concerns. Despite insistence, primarily by radical women of color or feminists of color, that constructions of gender are shaped by historical and cultural context, and that the notion of a universal femininity is fallacious, there does seem to be a predominant tendency to put forth totalizing conceptions of what consciousness, empowerment, and resistance entail. The "feminist," notwithstanding all this talk about context and anti-essentialism still stands as this generic figure. She may be sensitive to the multiple identities and subjectivities of the woman she writes about, aware of the nuances of sociopolitical processes that impact patriarchies, but she is generally positioned as someone who transcends it all.

Through an examination of my own shifting subjectivities in the research context, the intent is to expose the inadequacy of a one-dimensional feminist figure, and in doing so to highlight the linearity and Eurocentrism inherent in empowerment agendas in feminist research.

Episode Number 1

When I met Aisha in April 1992, she was trying to decide whether she wanted to adopt the *hijab* (the technical Arabic term for the Muslim veil) or not; and we had a series of lively discussions about the issue right after we met. These discussions sparked my curiosity, intellectual and otherwise, and helped me finalize the topic for the paper that eventually turned into my dissertation. We still continued our discussions, only now I took notes and taperecorded what transpired.

"I am a good Muslim in most ways," she once said, thoughtfully. "I am not dogmatic. I practice tolerance like the Holy Prophet said we should. I try to tell the truth. In other ways, too, I am fine. I don't cover my hair, though. I just like it so much."

She glanced fondly at the black mass that cascaded down almost to her waist. She had not braided it, and her hair was only restrained by a bandanna loosely knotted at the top of her head. The bandanna matched her red *shalwar kameez* and her bangles, and also my red *shalwar kameez*.[1] We were

---

[1] A *shalwar kameez* is the Pakistani national dress worn in other South Asian countries also. A *shalwar* is a baggy pair of trousers. A *kameez* is a tunic worn with the *shalwar*.

both dressed up as if we were all ready to go to a Pakistani birthday party. After some consideration, we had curbed our desires to deck ourselves as if we were going to a Pakistani wedding. It was Eid-ul-Azha, a major Islamic festival. It was also the last day of class for spring quarter 1992, June 9. We both played hookey, however, and after Aisha went to the Islamic Center in the morning for prayers, spent most of the day exploring the local dress stores, eating things we could not normally afford, and sitting on the university lawns talking.

I told her that I thought her hair was really beautiful, and she should not hide it. I was committed to the cause of persuading Aisha not to don the *hijab*. I did not want to collude in a process that I felt would disempower her.

"Yeah! But that is such a lame reason. I feel so superficial."

"No, that's not superficial. Your hair is part of who you are. And you like to see it and show it. I think that's okay," I countered. I did not want Aisha to give in to the oppression Islam had in store for women who totally submitted.

"So you are saying my hair is my identity. But I am more than my body parts. I am a person. I am a Muslim," she declared emphatically. "It is more important for me to express these identities."

"You said 'identities.' You used the plural. Your hair is part of this identity that involves presenting your physical beauty. You can have three identities," I mentally congratulated myself for the strategic use of Aisha's own words to respond to her argument.

"No, not when one of them comes in the way of the other two. People don't treat you like a person when they see you are an attractive female. And I can't tell God I like my hair!" She giggled. The drift of our conversation changed. I teased her about her lack of humility as far as her looks were concerned. She teased me back. And the afternoon passed.

Aisha started to cover her hair in front of *naamahram* men (men she could marry, according to Islamic law) in September 1992, when she came back to school after the summer vacation. She did not tell me about it, and when I met her outside the library for an interview session in early October I was speechless. All I asked was, "When?" I was genuinely upset. I was afraid she was going to lose her identity as a person. I also did not want her to be subjected to even more discriminatory treatment in educational settings.

Talking to her later in her apartment alleviated some of my anxiety. Aisha made it very clear it was her own choice. She seemed very sure. She was angry with her mother for actively opposing her decision.

"That's why I waited till I came here to put the *hijab* on for the first time. When I am already wearing it the next time I see her, it will be easier to take a stand. My mom is worried that no modem Pakistani Muslim boy would want to marry me. I can't understand why people get more concerned about *rishtas* (proposals) than pleasing God. And anyway, I want the guy who marries me to accept me the way I am. There must be someone who is like that out there, yes Lubna?"

I only listened. I had had no scruples about imposing my ideas on her earlier, but now that she had already taken the step I decided to be supportive. It was not just that I did not want to alienate her, I was beginning to be impressed by her strength and conviction.

It took me a while, 2 months 6 days to be precise, to acknowledge that I was actually beginning to understand her logic. It took me a year and 4 months to see her donning of the *hijab* as an act of creative resistance, an oppositional response to what she perceived as the undue emphasis on sexuality in the university environment around her. In empowering herself, Aisha provided me with fresh insights into the essentially context-bound nature of empowerment and reintroduced me to the subversive potential of the *hijab*. She contributed to the enrichment of my multiple selves: intellectual, academic, feminist, Muslim. So who was empowering whom in this case?

Episode Number 2

It was around 11 o'clock at night on February 11, 1993. 1 was getting ready to go to bed, having given up on making sense of a difficult text. I decided my capitulation was justified because I had spent 10 long tedious hours revising a grant proposal as part of my job as a research assistant. The telephone rang, and I picked up the receiver.

"Did I wake you up?" It was Fariha, sounding apologetic. "I am sorry, but I really need to talk to you. And you have to promise you won't tell my mother anything. If it is all right with you … " she said hesitantly.

I assured her that it was, expecting her to share news of another bad grade on a test. The week before, over the phone, I had helped Fariha with two makeup papers. She had not wanted her mother to know about her poor performance, so we had pretended to talk about world politics and its impact on Muslim lives, an issue dear to her mother's heart. Fariha did make it a point to mention Bosnia and Kashmir intermittently in order to alleviate my guilt.

School and grades, however, were not on Fariha's mind this evening. She launched into a rather complicated narrative about a quarrel with her mother, a recent letter from her father, and her decision to get married to the young man she loved. I asked her a few clarifying questions here and there. After she talked for a while, she suddenly asked me what she should do, adding that she counted on me to help her because I knew so much about the real world.

I was rather taken aback by her question. I was not prepared for the switch from the role of confidant to that of an adviser, at least in this instance. I had been flattered when, a few weeks ago in early January, Fariha trusted me enough to tell me about her secret love affair with this 19 year old young man who had recently moved to California from Pakistan. She had accidentally run into him outside her school sometime in November 1992, and they had fallen in love quite dramatically at first sight. I was extremely flattered when Fariha sent Razzaq to meet me at my department in the first week of February, in order to elicit my opinion. I was also thrilled when she told me that she did not mind me writing down her confidences as part of my fieldwork. Somehow, her insistence that my age and varied experiences bestowed on me a wisdom that made me an expert was neither flattering nor thrilling. I silently chided myself for being open to her about my divorce and my love life. I had been very selective in what I revealed to her, but I probably should have just abstained from the topic.

"So what should I do? What would you do if you were in my place?" Fariha repeated her query.

"Well," I began cautiously, "I wouldn't want to be married when I was 16 or 17, even 18, because I would want to finish my education."

"Well, I can do whatever I want when I am married to him," she responded. "In fact I will do it better, because I won't feel so alone. I will be with someone who understands me and will help me fulfill my ambitions."

And so began an intense 4 hour session in which I struggled to strike a balance between displaying consideration for Fariha's feelings toward this man, painting a bleak picture of a runaway marriage and its consequences, and ignoring my stress about the paper that I was supposed to start writing early next morning. We talked in Urdu, English, and Punjabi, and both of us drew from our multiple cultural bases to substantiate our reasoning. I, however, gradually became aware that my predominant persona was that of an older sister wanting to protect the little one from the clutches of an unsuitable man. Much to my horror, this older sister also wanted to run to the mother to get her help, even as she kept on promising Fariha that she would never disclose her secret. I respected and admired Fariha's mother. In the few months that I had known her I had become quite close to her. I called her *Appa*, which means older sister.

What I could gather from Fariha's outpouring that night was that Appa had found out about this young man in Fariha's life and had forbidden her to ever see him again. She had behaved, in my opinion, somewhat unreasonably. I could see why she did not want Fariha to be involved with the man. But she had really made Fariha angry by comparing her to her father, and threatening to send her off either to stay with him or live with his parents in Pakistan. After her outburst, Appa had locked herself up in her room.

I delicately suggested to Fariha that she try to talk to her mother. I offered to come over and be the mediator. After all, that seemed to be my predominant role in their lives. Fariha resolutely turned down the proposal.

Finally, we reached a point in the conversation where I felt that I had persuaded Fariha to put off her plan for at least a week. She was still adamant about wanting to get married as soon as possible, but decided to give me a chance to come up with a plan that was likely to have less disastrous consequences. Restating my promise not to tell her mother about our conversation, I hung up and drifted off into a restless sleep.

I spent a lot of time in the next 2 days trying to figuring out my course of action. I attempted to thrash out the issue with my colleagues and friends. Mostly, these attempts were a waste of time, because people seemed to be more interested in criticizing Muslims for not allowing their daughters to choose their partners than in offering me advice. A few friends, however, did present their point of view succinctly.

Away from Fariha and her mother, back in my academic world, the simplicity of the logic employed by these friends appealed to my distraught mind. I decided that my guilt at breaching Appa's trust was misplaced. My first commitment was toward Fariha and her desires. Fariha was 17, and by Islamic standards an adult. She could marry anyone she wanted. I would neither divulge her secret nor force my ideas on her. I would respect her choice and be supportive no matter what she did.

When I got home from the library on the 14th of February, there were six frantic messages from Appa on my answering machine. I immediately called her back. Fariha had run away. She had left a letter for her mother. Appa had decided to tell people that she was staying with me. Only her youngest brother, one of Fariha's maternal uncles knew the truth. Appa told me that the least I could do for her and Fariha was to back up her lie, because my negative influence on Fariha was to a large extent responsible for her elopement.

Fariha had told me where she would go if she ran away. Appa's pain was hard for me to bear but I forced myself not to say anything. I knew I would find it very difficult to maintain my confidentiality in Appa's presence, so I tried to stay away from her as much as possible.

Nonetheless, both Appa and Fariha's uncle realized I knew more than I admitted. When Appa contacted Fariha's father in desperation, and he almost took the other children away, her uncle practically begged me to help look for her. I eventually gave in, and using the information I gave him, he traced her whereabouts. He could not meet her physically but sent her a message telling her at least to let them know where she was.

Fariha came back to her mother's place after a week, all by herself, in very bad shape. She looked haggard, and seemed to have bruises on her face. She told her mother that she had received her uncle's message. She had gone through the *nikah* (the Muslim legal marriage) with Razzaq, but she wanted help in getting it annulled. Her mother brought Fariha over to my place, and she stayed with me for about 2 weeks while her mother and uncle arranged for the *nikah* to be declared void. She was very quiet, and lost in a world of her own. We barely communicated. I saw her crying on and off

The sequence of happenings, Fariha's running away, her coming back, and my involvement in these, have assumed a nightmarish quality in my memory. My reflective journal and field note entries constantly remark on the "unreal nature of the experience." The most authentic part of the whole episode for me was the rhetorical question Appa posed to me at one point when I was still mired in issues of confidentiality, choice, and agency; "What if this had happened to your own sister?"

Yes, what if it were my own sister instead of Fariha? Would I not have thought of words other than "confidentiality," "choice," and "agency," words that I cannot translate into English? In my initial interactions with Fariha, in my attempt to have access to data, I was interested in mobilizing my hybrid identity. For instance, I got into the older sister mode with Fariha quite smoothly because of our shared Punjabi ethnicity. When it came to defining empowerment for Fariha, I could set myself apart from the cultural bridge that connected me to her family. Choosing to ally my-self with my Western modes of thought, I became the "feminist." In de-taching myself from my subjectivity as a Pakistani Muslim woman, from my familial relationship with Fariha, my attempts at reciprocity contributed to the perpetuation of Eurocentric binarism, whereby the "objective" is privi-leged over the "subjective."

CLOSING REMARKS

These two episodes illustrate that unless agendas of empowerment are seen as arising from the specificity of women's lives and experiences, feminism becomes another hegemonic system of meaning. Aisha is covering herself up, curtailing the expression of her personality; but according to her stance, her personality derives from a collectivity, the Muslim *umma* (transnational Islamic community), and the *hijab* becomes a signifier of her participation in that collectivity. From one perspective, Fariha's action is not "feminist" enough. She runs away in order to "resist" family restrictions and an un-friendly if not outright hostile school environment, but she runs to a man and even marries him in a very patriarchal ceremony. Yet her romance con-tinues the age-old tradition of thought from the Indian subcontinent, which puts forth heterosexual love as a subversive force, corroding the dominant order for which segregation of sexes serves as a mechanism of control. Her mother's expectations of her, academically and otherwise, also need to be framed within her life's circumstances and her perceived threat from the mainstream cultural systems.

I wish I had the space to go into a detailed analysis of the power regimes impacting my subjectivity, in order to elaborate further on the ambiguity of conceptions of empowerment underlining feminist research in education and other contexts. Notions such as "catalytic validity" and "conscientization" posit the idea that an authentic, fixed, absolute consciousness is possible, and by implication the feminist or critical researcher becomes the bearer of this asset. My last question is: In fostering the illusion of the "know-it-all" researcher, is critical research, feminist or otherwise, surpassing the oppressive conditions of so-called traditional research contexts?

REFERENCES

Freire, P. (1970). *Pedagogy of the oppressed.*. New York: Continuum

Lather, P. (1991). *Getting smart: Feminist research and pedagogy with/in the postmodern.* New York: Routledge.

4

An African American Female Researcher's Journey: Epistemological, Conceptual, and Methodological Concerns

Arlette Ingram Willis
University of Illinois at Urbana-Champaign

In some very important epistemological ways, I have been preparing to write this chapter all of my life, drawing on my life experiences of being African American, female, and middle class. That is, I have known for a long time, to paraphrase Dionne Farris' (1994) song, *Human*[*]:

> Before I am black
> Before I am woman
> Before I am short
> Before I am young
> Before I am African
> I am Human

In other ways, there is no possibility I would have been able to write this chapter until now.

Several years ago, like many assistant professors, I began looking for outlets for my dissertation shortly after graduation and after accepting a tenure-track position at a major research institution. Initially, there were no takers for a critical historical study of reading comprehension test development and test developers in the United States from 1910 to 1919. It did not take long for it to occur to me that I had been operating under the naive assumption that notions of the hegemonic forces which supported and maintained the status quo were known, but not accepted within the academy. Over time, it became clear to me that it was not just my study that was being rejected, it was who was telling the story, that is, the point of view that I represented through my telling.

My ideal of being a good researcher and being a good writer quickly gave way to the harsh reality of writing for an audience that did not want to be offended or challenged to address issues of race, class, gender, and power relations in the forming of institutions and policies regarding literacy testing. It became very clear to me that what gets published about issues of race, class, and gender in professional literacy journals is still very much a part of the issues of power and domination within specialized fields and education in general. Toni Morrison (1992) referred to this phenomenon as "writing for a white audience." She acknowledges the dilemma and queries: "What happens to the writerly imagination of a black author who is at some level *always* conscious of representing one's own race to, or in spite of, a race of readers that understands itself to be 'universal' or race-free?" (p. xii).

The rejections of my work, however, also taught me a far more important lesson. The rejections although hard to swallow at the time, allowed me to understand the importance of presenting my viewpoints, as an informed African American female researcher, without regrets. The process of conducting research as an African American female within the specialized areas of the history of literacy and literacy education, which traditionally have been dominated and characterized by Euro-American males and in which the histories and experiences of non-Whites and women have been suppressed, encouraged me to adopt a clearer sense of vision and direction. I struggled, nevertheless, with finding my academic voice or writing in a manner that was both a part of who I am and responsive to the academic traditions of scholarly publications.

During my daily prayer and meditation time, I sought the Lord's help on how to translate my viewpoints and research into text. The interpretation of this step, of seeking spiritual aid and support, should not be taken lightly. The role of spirituality in the lives of some researchers and in research, especially in research conducted about and by people of color, where it is central, is often overlooked and unacknowledged (Stanfield, 1994). Shortly thereafter, I was attending a national conference, when, out of the corner of my eye, I caught sight of a flyer announcing a session at which Sonia Sanchez was speaking. I rushed to the session to hear her. As I found a seat and settled into the session, I recalled a similar moment in my life, over 20 years earlier, when as an undergraduate I sat listening to her on a college campus. The memory of this African American woman, reading her poetry—poetry so powerful that it captured the attention and silenced an auditorium of African American undergraduates—came rushing back. Sanchez read her work with such compassion and empathy. She eloquently retold the historic plight and oppression of African American women, within and outside of the academy. Her spell over the audience was broken, however, when she addressed the relationships between African American males and females. As she proclaimed the virtues of Black males, she said with flair, "They don't know how easy they are!" The room erupted as African American women jumped and shouted in affirmation. It seemed as if she had "read" and articulated our world, our thoughts, and our emotions. It was so empowering to have been there, to have seen and heard her, to have experienced what it felt like to be proud of being African American and female in a less-than-welcoming environment of higher education.

In 1995, I was still moved by her poetry, as were the rest of the people, mostly women, who attended her session. Sanchez read with such passion, such depth, such empathy, and such caring that many wept over her words. In fact, after she completed her readings, the chair of the session called for a break so that members of the panel could compose themselves enough to continue the session. Without asking, she spoke to my struggle to have my voice heard within academia. Her advice, to me and others, came in a response to a query from someone in the audience. Sanchez observed, "The very best writing comes when you write about something you are passionate about." I held on to these words, as they helped me to understand better the voice that was missing in my work. Sanchez continued by asking, "If you cannot write passionately about a topic, why write at all?" It was clear to me that my writing lacked passion.

In retrospect, I could see how my unpublished manuscripts had consisted of mechanically filling in a mythical academic outline I believed would lead to a scholarly publication. They were not a reflection of my way of knowing or interpreting the world around me. My voice was missing; I had tried to acquire the voice and viewpoints espoused in the literature I had read. Sanchez's comments had challenged me to ask myself, "What do I feel passionately about?" Among other things, I was passionate about the historic and contemporary barriers to literacy experienced by many African Americans in the United States, and the literacy education that my three African American sons were or were not receiving in school. I wondered, however, how I was to write passionately about history or to write passionately about the literacy education for children of color in a system designed to deny their existence and thwart their voices? I had come a long way; I had begun to define my areas of interest. Now, I needed to determine how I would go about reaching my goals.

Encouraged as I had become by the wisdom and words of Sanchez, I still lacked a conceptual framework for thinking about and conducting research among members of my own community. The ideological notions of Antonio Gramsci (1971) and Paulo Freire (1970) came close to capturing my thinking, but they lacked a sociohistorical understanding of the interconnectedness of race, class, gender, and power oppression as experienced by African American women in the United States. At no time in my professional preparation had I been introduced to, nor had I happened on Black feminist thought. However, through some independent research, I found my epistemological and conceptual home.

African American Feminist/Womanist Thought

The work of Patricia Hill Collins (1990) helped me to understand why my viewpoints were more than mere alternatives to Western, Eurocentric, male-dominated epistemologies. The work of African American feminists/womanists was grounded in a way of knowing and interpreting the world that did not use White middle-class male/female experiences as the norm. African American feminist/womanist writings argued that there were ways of viewing the world—ways that do not use, as Lorde (1995) suggested, "the master's tools."—and that we, African American women, had a unique view of the world—a view born out of a history of race, class, and gender oppression that helped to shape our ways of knowing and interpreting the world. This is not to say that all African American women have the same experiences or that we are all alike. What these theories do say is that for many African American women, how we make meaning of the world around us represents as valid a way of knowing and interpreting the world as other epistemologies that do not include our views. Moreover, we can legitimately contextualize the settings, experiences, voices, and outcomes within an African American feminist/womanist perspective that reflect our cultural, collective, and personal histories.

The brilliant essay "The social construction of Black feminist thought," by Patricia Hill Collins (1995) has been republished in Beverly Guy-Sheftall's *Words of Fire*. She writes, "expressing a black feminist consciousness is problematic precisely because more powerful groups have a vested interest in suppressing such thought … thereby establishing their view of reality as superior to alternative interpretations" (pp. 339–341). Hill Collins also argues that rearticulating the standpoint of African American women through black feminist thought is much more difficult since one cannot use the same techniques to study the knowledge of the dominated as one uses to study the knowledge of the powerful. This is precisely because subordinate groups have long had to use alternative ways to create an independent consciousness. (pp. 341)

Finally, in this essay she suggests several requirements for the acceptance of Black feminist thought: its growth from the experiences of and validation of the experiences of ordinary women, acceptance by scholars in the field of Black feminist thought, and willingness to confront White male viewpoints (Hill Collins, 1995).

The most meaningful source for me has been Patricia Hill Collins's *Black Feminist Thought* (1990). In this work, Hill Collins described four distinct dimensions of African American women's ways of interpreting reality: (a) concrete experience as a criterion for meaning, (b) the use of dialogue in assessing knowledge claims, (c) the ethic of caring, and (d) the ethic of personal accountability (pp. 208–219). I have included a brief summary of each consideration in the paragraph following.

The first consideration is the importance of knowledge and knowing based on experience. Hill Collins (1990) writes that "for most African American women, those individuals who have lived through the experiences about which they claim to be experts are more believable and credible than those who have merely read or thought about such experiences" (Collins, 1990, p. 209). Second is the importance of the use of dialogue to assess knowledge claims. Hill Collins articulates the importance of dialogue as follows "For Black women new knowledge claims are rarely worked out in isolation from other individuals and are usually developed through dialogues with other members of a community" (p.212). She also quotes bell hooks (1989) who noted that "dialogue implies talk between two subjects, not the speech of subject and object. It is a humanizing speech, one that challenges and resists domination" (p. 131). Third Hill Collins evokes the importance of caring, stating that "the value placed on individual expressiveness, the appropriateness of emotions, and the capacity for empathy are central to the knowledge validation process"(p. 216). Hill Collins (1990) writes that within an ethic of personal accountability, "people are expected to be accountable for their knowledge claims" (p. 218). Or, as Gloria Ladson-Billings (1994) has interpreted Hill Collins' notion of an ethic of personal accountability, it implies "both *what* was said and *who* said it give meaning and interpretation to claims" (p.156).

These days, I conceptualize my work by acknowledging my connection to the articulation of African American feminist/womanist epistemologies through the scholarly efforts of women who have had the strength of character to challenge White male and female notions of knowing, and who present alternative African American feminist/womanist epistemologies. Moreover, I have begun to read the epistemological positions of other women researchers of color. These latter epistemologies acknowledge the historic and contemporary manifestations of oppression and marginalization that move ways of knowing and interpreting the world beyond simplistic notions of biological and racial inheritance. Research, so understood, adds breadth and depth to the intellectual community.

The writings of African American female scholars and theorists became important resources for me as I was developing my "academic" voice. As bell hooks (1994) observed, "Without our voices in written work and in oral presentations there will be no articulation of our concerns" (p. 105). Gwen Etter-Lewis (1993) describes the presence of African American women in the academy this way:

> The notion that African American women are an invisible group on the sidelines that easily can be combined with other groups is a convenient fiction that conceals their power and importance. They have played major roles in all of American culture and continue to do so in spite of resistance and a variety of formidable barriers. (p. xvii)

It was important to me to understand where I fit and where my research fits within a larger history of African American women. For that, I made a personal search of works written by African American women detailing the history of African American Women in America.

A History of African American Women

As frustrating as my personal journey had become, I was aware of the pathway created by countless known and unknown African American women who throughout history had actively fought against race, gender, and class oppression: Anna Julia Cooper, Alice Dunbar-Nelson, Frances E. W. Harper, Claudia Jones, Floreynce Kennedy, Mary Church Terrell, Sojourner Truth, Harriet Tubman, and Ida Wells-Barnett, to name a few. The views held by African American women continue to echo the words of Anna Julia Cooper, who in 1892 observed that:

> One muffled strain in the Silent South, a jarring chord and a vague and uncomprehended cadenza has been and still is the Negro. And of that muffled chord, the one mute and voiceless note has been the sadly expectant Black Woman ... The "other side" has not been represented by one who "lives there." And not many can sensibly realize and more accurately tell the weight and the fret of the "long dull pain" than the open-eyed but hitherto voiceless Black Woman of America.. (Lemert & Bahn, p. 51)

The lives and accomplishments of pioneering African American women, were not a part of my professional training and preparation within a White male dominated research university. Their accomplishments and writing were not part of the curriculum or the research that mattered to my instructors. Nor was the more recent scholarship of Patricia Bell-Scott, Angela Davis, Beverly Guy-Sheftall, Patricia Hill Collins, Darlene Clark Hine, bell hooks, Audre Lorde, Pauli Murray, Linda Perkins, Barbara Smith, and Alice Walker, among others, acknowledged. However, the research and writings of these women became another source of reference, hope, and inspiration.

Along with the lives and accomplishments of these activists and scholars, I must acknowledge the equally important lives and accomplishments of the unheralded African American women, including my foremothers, who from their first days in this land have "done more than find ways to feed a family with little or nothing in the house. They have found ways to educate children, resist the oppressions of slavery, support their churches, build hospitals, register voters, and get elected to the United States Senate. Theirs is more than a story of oppression and struggle. It is a story of hope" (Hine & Thompson, 1998, pp. 5–6).

Darlene Clark Hine and Kathleen Thompson's beautifully written book *A Shining Thread of Hope: The History of Black Women in America* (1998) offers an important timeline for understanding the histories of African American women in this country and the oppressions they have endured and triumphs they have accomplished. The authors list several themes that emerged from their writing of an African American woman's history: an emphasis on community, education as a priority, the importance of understanding individual self-worth, and triumph over obstacles. Like many others, they note that African American women have historically been faced with the simultaneous oppressive forces of race, class, and gender, which have made their struggle very different from the struggle of African American males and White women. Hine and Thompson observe that the unique position of African American women throughout "life and history, made most Black women *de facto* feminist"s (p. 313).

PUBLISHING HISTORIES AND LITERACIES OF AFRICAN AMERICANS

The road from conceptualization to research to writing to publication still remains a minefield for women of color, especially when they conduct research within their community. Anna Julia Cooper (1902), writing nearly a century ago, cleverly captured the process when she wrote:

In the old days, I am told that two or three Negroes gathered together in supplication and prayer, were not allowed to present their petition at the throne of Grace without having it looked over and revised by a white man for fear probably that white supremacy and its "peculiar" system might be endangered at the Court of the Almighty by these faltering lips and uncultured tongues! The same fear cowers the white man's heart today. He dare not face his God with a lie on his lips. (Lemert & Bhan, 1997, p. 214)

In academic circles, this marginalization is known as "institutional silencing" (Gitlin, 1994, p. 4). Whether conscious or not, it silences our voices through the lack of recognition by our peers. It is greater than the failure to have our work acknowledged; it suggests that our work is not taken seriously, especially when it is research that emerges from within our communities. The remainder of this chapter describes some of the methodological concerns I have encountered while conducting research among my community and while reading about research conducted by European Americans within African American communities. The chapter ends with a call to broaden conceptual frameworks for literacy research among people of color.

One of my research projects found me interviewing elderly African American people who had attended a private, independent boarding school in rural Alabama. I had learned about the school and its existence from relatives. For several years, I conducted preliminary background research on the school and found that none of the researchers had interviewed former school administrators, teachers, or students to learn of their experiences at the school. The school was immensely popular among the members of the African American community, so I thought interviewing former students might be one way of shedding light on why African Americans considered it an excellent school in which to enroll their children and what we could learn from them about creating quality learning environments for African American children. Several of the former students, males in their late 70s and 80s, were most helpful and shared with me at length their experiences at Calhoun. One gentleman, Walter Morris, was particularly helpful. He made a special trip to the reunion, traveling from California, for the opportunity to share his experiences at Calhoun with me for my research project. He also brought several artifacts with him that I copied. After the interviews were completed and transcribed, all of the interviewees read through the transcriptions and returned their copies with additions and corrections. Thus, although some of the local folks in the rural African American community were not as forthcoming as I had hoped they would be, many others who had attended Calhoun shared with me their life stories as well as their memories and experiences of attending Calhoun Colored School.

I arranged an interview with the oldest living alumna of the school, Leona Lee. Mrs. Lee was 104 and living with her daughter, Juliette, a spry 80-year-old, in Camarillo, CA. I followed the prescribed protocols for gaining entrée, identifying myself as a university professor and describing the focus of my research—to learn about Mrs. Lee's experiences as a student at Calhoun Colored School. Although she was polite, it was clear that Juliette was cautiously guarding her mother and her privacy from the caller at the other end of the phone. I decided to "locate" myself for them; that is, I informed them that my aunt had attended the school. This was a subtle but clear message to them that I was an African American woman who was interested in learning more about the experiences of African American students who had attended Calhoun, and that my interest was both personal and professional. On learning of my familial connections and my interest beyond publications, Juliette's guard came down a little. There was still skepticism in her voice about allowing a stranger into her home and her mother's life. Eventually, I was invited to their home in Camarillo for an interview.

We had agreed on a date and time, and I traveled to California to conduct the interview. The agreed-on date was a Sunday morning, roughly 12:00 noon, after Leona and her daughter had returned from church. (They attend church faithfully every Sunday morning, and although I was welcomed, my schedule needed to coincide with their routine.) Having grown up under very similar circumstances, I completely understood their desires and complied by their wishes. The morning of the interview I began to recall, unconsciously at first, then consciously, the many dos and don'ts of my childhood.

My parents, both raised in the South, had trained me in all the cultural expectations of a "proper child" since I was a toddler. The training consisted of the grooming and preparation of a young woman, as my mother and maternal grandmother (two forerunners to Ms. Manners) deemed important. In some ways their ideas were almost Victorian, but I understood that their training was an important part of what they believed I needed to know. One of the many important lessons I learned was to know and understand my *place* among elderly folk—one of unquestioned respect and honor.

My early training also helped me to anticipate cultural expectations that these elderly women, both professional women, born in the South, might have of an African American researcher. (It is not clear to me that they would have held the same expectations for a White male or female researcher.) For example, I knew that I needed to be modest in my appearance: wearing seasonably appropriate, well-cared for clothes; applying light lipstick and makeup; moisturizing every exposed body part; and wearing a flattering but modest hairdo.

The first impression these women had of me, and how they would then *locate* me within their realm of expectations for an African American scholar, had little to do with university degrees. My personal grooming and deportment would speak volumes to them of who my parents were and whether or not they had raised me in a manner that was proper. I was to be pleasant, patient, and helpful at every turn. I was not expected to be waited on, but to offer to assist them. The early training of my parents, so much of which I took for granted, was now very important as a means of entrée into their world, a world very similar to that of my grandparents and parents.

I arrived right on time; being too early would have been considered rude. Juliette answered the door and was carefully assured that I was nonthreatening. As I handed her the flowers I had purchased, she greeted me warmly and led me through the house to a sunny spot in the backyard where Leona was sitting.

Leona did not look like the 104-year-old woman I had imagined. She was an elderly light-skinned woman with gray hair, bedecked with pearls, still dressed for church. She sat poised but comfortable awaiting me. As I greeted her, I could hardly believe that I was talking with someone so old who spoke clearly and articulately. She informed me, quite proudly, that today, as she does every Sunday, she had washed and pressed her hair before attending church. (I was impressed; even with a perm I seldom went to that much trouble before church.) We chatted briefly before she said she needed to move out of the sun. I understood this as my queue to offer assistance and follow any specific requests she made about how and where she wanted to sit.

As the interview moved along, Leona appeared more relaxed and chatted on endlessly about her days at Calhoun. This incredible woman sang me the school prayer she had learned while attending Calhoun as a teenager. She told me about her on-campus duties and being the valedictorian of her class. (Juliette later sent me a copy of her speech.) She also shared stories, recollections, and memories of her early years as a schoolteacher in a one-room day school run by Calhoun.

As the interview session continued, Juliette made frequent visits to check on us and offer us refreshments. The 2 hour interview had turned into a day visit with these delightful women. They provided me with a tour of their home and shared family stories, photos, and mementos. After my third offer of Ensure, I realized it was time to eat, so we went out for dinner followed by a tour of the city. Later, we made photocopies of some of Leona's many awards and plaques. Throughout the interview, Juliette and Leona answered my questions and often provided information that they felt was important for me to know about Calhoun and Leona's experiences. We have kept in touch ever since.

Being African American and female does not mean instant entrée, however, into the community and lives of African American people. My early experience with the elderly women in California did not prepare me for a less-than-positive experience in the rural South. My next set of interviews for this project took me to the school district superintendent's office, the school, the current staff, and the president of the national alumni association.

My mother and aunt who were born and raised in the area, escorted me on the first set of interviews in the South. My aunt, who lives in a large city, served as a tour guide and gatekeeper into the African American community in the small rural town in which the school is located. Her presence was greatly appreciated when I met with the superintendent and with the alumni association president. Both the superintendent and the alumni president were never very forthcoming with information about the school. I shared my frustration with my aunt, who quickly began to call on sorority sisters (the same sorority to which the president of the alumni association belonged) to gain further access to the school and alumni in the area. This was a wake-up call for me. Naively, I had assumed that being African American, with parents from the South and an aunt who had attended the Calhoun Colored School, would give me easy access to the site and welcomed entrée to interviews. I learned that although I was African American, I was viewed as an outsider: I was not from the South, I was not a "Calhoun" person, and I was not a member of the immediate African American community.

Several months later, I returned to the area for the Calhoun National Alumni Association's annual reunion. I had contacted many of the attendees in advance and made arrangements for interviews during the reunion. In addition, I located myself with them by telling them a little about my family from the area and my interest in the research project. Most attendees seemed to welcome the opportunity to share their experiences at Calhoun with me. Some, on learning that I was a member of a respected family within the larger African American community, were very helpful in sharing their time, memories, and artifacts with me.

One of the most important lessons I learned from this experience was that being an African American does not mean you have instant access into an African American community. My aunt's intercession into the African American community's network helped me to gain further acceptance and access to individuals than I could have gained on my own. Another important lesson I learned is that the cultural nuances I have so often taken for granted were brought to a heightened sense of consciousness as I attempted to negotiate with elderly African Americans and African Americans who lived in a very different geographical community. I was ever mindful of all the "lessons" of deportment as well as the cultural expectations, some beyond words, that my parents had instilled within me. I also recalled their warnings about becoming an "educated fool." I understood their caution was due in part from their own sense of parenting, and in part because they knew I would need to know how to survive within an African American community. Finally, I learned about the details of the lives of many of the interviewees. Their descriptions of the lives of their parents, as well as their own lives, after the turn-of-the-century offered me a rich and varied account of each of the interviewees. Moreover, while they all attended Calhoun, their experiences at the school differed as well. This new information allowed me to understand the importance of shared dialogue, a sense of caring, respect for the individual's experience, and the importance of my responsibility to write and share their accounts of their experiences in a meaningful way. I became ever more sensitive to the importance of not essentializing their experiences under some notion of rural African American poor. I wanted to write and share their stories with the passion they conveyed and as part of the oral history of the South.

The experience also helped me to read my world of literacy differently. I could no longer sit idly by as European American researchers attempted to portray African American children, adults, and learners in their studies in monolithic terms, as flat characters in "their" research projects. This experience leads me to my next methodological understanding.

Literacy Research in the African American Community

At a recent national literacy conference, I was dismayed as a well-respected White female researcher shared how enlightening an experience it had been for her to revisit some of her earlier research among African American children, and how rich those memories are for her. As she recalled her interviews with African American girls, and their attention or inattention to the research interventions, I found myself wondering what those little girls might have looked like. Considering the years in which the research projects were undertaken, I pictured a preadolescent African American girl neatly dressed with Sista curls, not the Shirley Temple curls I wore at a similar age. (The hairstyling process, on virgin hair, for creating both kind of curls is similar.)

I can still vividly recall my excitement about "getting my hair done," by someone other than my mother, who would make me look like Shirley Temple. Though now I am bothered by the label of "Shirley Temple curls," I do not recall it as an attempt to "look White" but rather an attempt to capture the cherub-like image of innocence portrayed by Shirley Temple and promoted by the mass media.

Like the other little girls who attended the African Methodist Episcopal church in my hometown, having Shirley Temple curls meant you had endured hours of having someone "work" with your virgin (unprocessed) hair. Your hair first had to be washed and dried. Later, it was straightened and curled. The entire process took hours. Your job was to endure the process in silence as your mother chatted with the hairdresser about world events and local gossip. Even when your little legs stuck to the chair's plastic cover or the stack of telephone books used to prop you up so the hairdresser would not have to strain to straighten and curl your hair, you were to sit without complaining. Once in a while you might drift off to sleep—then, the hairdresser would bring the straighten comb close to your skin or you would feel the sizzling hot hair oil burn your scalp, suddenly, you would awake from your slumber with a start.

For me, this special hairstyle usually occurred before a seasonal holiday at which my parents wanted me to look extra special when we went to church. After early morning church service, we would go home and return later for the children's program. This is when all the Sunday School children performed their special speeches/Bible verses and classroom plays. These days, however, little African American girls can wear Sista curls daily and do not have to wait for a holiday.

The researcher had not mentioned anything about the participants in her study other than that they were African American girls, as if that somehow summarized their lives. She did not report anything about them other than age and race. For example, there are cultural insights behind how the girls' hair was styled: if the girls' hair was straightened, permed, frizzy; or if the girls wore their hair straight or in Sista curls; or if the girls had one, two, three, braids or more. Hairstyles are just one of many cultural markers that could have added some insight into the lives of these girls outside of the classroom and research sites.

This discussion is not about hairstyles, but about the knowledge that researchers bring to research. Intuitively, I know and bring different knowledge to the research among members of my own community that is meaningful, insightful and informative. What concerns me here is that the researcher who was reporting her data in a retrospective did not acknowledge any lack of insight about the context or about the girls. This researcher's ability to "objectify the differences" (Anzaldua. 1990, p. xxi) between herself, as a White researcher, and the African American girls was problematic for me. It was as if she felt entitled to place a thin white veneer over the lives of the African American girls in "her research project." She had missed a significant portion of their stories, which in turn made her research only a shadow of their lives. Her failure to acknowledge, or to cite, the work of African American researchers who have conducted research within our own communities, also was unfortunate. After years of such published research, she remained wedded to the ideas and insights of other White researchers. Her prominence in the field suggests that others will also continue to cite her work as "good research" among African Americans because she followed outlined steps and procedures despite the fact that she failed to consider the young African American girls in her research as anything other than flat stereotypical images of personhood, missing the dynamic complexity of their lives.

Like Gloria Anzaldua (1990), I argue that this particular researcher's lack of positioning suggests that we insiders should be concerned about "the ways knowledges are invented. It means continually challenging institutionalized discourses. It means being suspicious of the dominant culture's interpretations of 'our' experience of the way they 'read' us" (p. xxv).

On the one hand, I wondered if I was being unfair. How could this White woman researcher possibly understand the many layers of context that were operating when she thought she was merely conducting a research project? On the other hand, I feel justified in challenging her lack of in-depth descriptions and portrayal of the African American girls in her study without consideration of the larger sociohistorical context in which these girls were living. Why shouldn't I challenge her ability to contextualize the environment more completely? Spina and Tai (1998) have argued that

> not seeing race is predicated on not seeing White as race and in denying Whiteness as a focus of critique and analysis. Ignoring the racial construction of Whiteness reinscribes its centrality and reinforces its privilege and oppressive position as normative. (p. 37)

In addition, Lorde (1995) observed that

> there are very real differences between us of race, age, and sex. But it is not those differences between us that are separating us. It is rather our refusal to recognize those differences, and to examine the distortions that result from our misnaming them and their effects upon human behavior and expectations. (p. 285)

I wondered how much more she could have grown if she had allowed her understanding to be informed by the research of African Americans who had conducted similar studies among African American children.

Literacy Research Among Our Own

How do we read ourselves? Below is a vignette drawn from my own research (Willis, 1995) that helps to illustrate how I interpreted my son's experience and how others "read" the experience. Let me share a conversation that I had with my 9-year-old son, and the context in which it occurred:

It's a cold frosty winter morning and everyone has left for work or school except my youngest son, Jake, and me. I am busy applying last minute touches and encouraging Jake, in the next room, to "step it up." I wonder why is he dragging around. School starts in 10 minutes and we haven't left the house. He knows the routine; I wonder if something is troubling him. So, I peek around the corner and find him forlorn—you know, scowl on his face, a look of growing despair and sadness. I forget about the clock and attend to him.

I ask, "Jake what's wrong? Why are you so unhappy?"

"We have the Young Authors [writing] Contest today, and I don't have anything to write about."

"Sure you do. There are lots of things you can write about ," I encourage him. (I think people write best about those subjects they know and care about.) Why don't you write about baseball or soccer?"

"No," he replies. "A kid at our school wrote about cancer last year and the story went all the way to the next state [regionals]."

"Well," I answer, "maybe you should write about something funny—like when you go to the barbershop. You and your brothers are always talking about your trips there."

"Oh no, Mom, they wouldn't understand. When I just get my haircut, they always ask me, "Why do you have that line in your hair?" It's not a line, it's a part, I try to tell them. I can't write about the barbershop. They won't understand."

"Well," I say, trying to clarify what I really mean, "I don't mean write about getting a haircut. I mean writing about all the funny people that come in and the things that happen while you are at the barbershop. You and your brothers always come home tellin' a funny story and laugh about it for the rest of the week. That's what I mean by tell them about the barbershop."

"No, Mom, they won't understand," he insists.

"What do you mean, 'they' won't understand? Who is this 'they?'" I ask.

"The people in my class," he replies, somewhat frustrated.

Jake continues: "You should read this story that M. wrote. It is a mystery story and it's really good. I can't beat that story. I'll bring you a copy of it if I can. I know it will win." (Sadder now that he has had time to consider his competition, he turns and walks toward his room.)

Wanting him to participate, I ask, "How do you know M's story is good?"

"She read it in class. Everybody said it's really good," he responds.

"Well, I still think you should try. You are a really good writer. Look at all the 'good stuff' you wrote in Mrs. S's room. You could rewrite some of it and turn it in."

Finally, he answers, "I'll think about it." Then, we are off to school. (pp. 30–49)

I have offered in this vignette, as an intimate look into the home, family, and community of one African American family. Few Euro-American researchers, regardless of their research viewpoints, concepts, and theories, will ever be able to capture a similar insight with multifaceted meanings that come from an insider's intimate relationship to historic and contemporary individual and collective experiences.

What I surmise from this vignette is simply that if the cultural oppression of school literacy practices is clear to a 9-year-old African American child, it should also be clear to learned scholars and researchers. My guess is that they were probably clear to him earlier, but he lacked the ability to articulate what he was beginning to understand were the unstated rules of school literacy success. The vignette is not the data you find in most professional journals, because this is the real stuff, the in your house, behind closed doors, stuff of conversation in families and worries of African American parents. Except for minor changes suggested during publication, the vignette has not filtered through the lens of a researcher who has little knowledge of the family history, home, and community contexts, as well as the literacy history of this young man. There are few reports in literacy that describe the extent to which children from culturally and linguistically diverse backgrounds understand the process of school literacy. Why? Race, class, and gender marginalization in academia, often veiled by explanations of blind/peer reviews, retain power, privilege, and prestige in the hands of a few—few of whom are African American females, as they review manuscripts for publication.

The vignette thus offers an alternative view and analysis of school literacy practices. In so doing, it defies the generic theories of school literacy that suggest that all children will come to warm, welcoming school environments where teachers are knowledgeable and accepting of cultural and linguistic differences. Other women researchers of color in the field of literacy espouse similar positions. For example, Reyes (1992) has observed that failing to account for cultural, linguistic, or individual differences in literacy theory has led to a "one size does fit all" mentality. Furthermore, she argues that teachers use theories and strategies based upon research with mainstream populations, hoping that "the high rate of success with process instruction reported for mainstream students will magically happen for culturally and linguistically diverse learners" (pp. 436–437), and adopting a position that presumes that "African American children are exactly like white children but just need a little extra help" (Ladson-Billings, 1994, p. 9).

I have found it very interesting to listen to my European American colleagues' interpretations of the above vignette. Most often, I have been congratulated for the fine article "about my son." I am amused by their responses, as I did not envision the vignette or the article as merely an intimate insider view of one African American family's response to the literacy education of their child. No, I have always considered it to be a statement about the cultural and racial assumptions inherent in the theory and practice of school literacy. My crafting of the article included reiterations of the concerns of African American leaders throughout the century who have articulated their concerns about the forced duality of consciousness that African American children come to understand and learn to adopt in order to be "successful" in school. It seems, in some sense, that I have come full circle, knocking on the academy door, waiting for someone to hear and heed the call to open their eyes, ears, and hearts to multiple realities, theories, perspectives, and sources of knowledge.

My journey continues down a pathway to find and reconcile who I am, what I bring to the academy as an African American female researcher. Far beyond finding my voice, now I see the need to challenge the status quo, especially in literacy research, that continues to ignore, marginalize, and silence voices like mine. As Dionne Farris (1944) wrote in her song, *Human:*

> Because I am black
> Because I am woman
> Because I am short
> Because I am African
> I am Human

REFERENCES

Andulza, G., (Ed.). (1990). *Making face, making soul (haciendo caras): Creative and critical perspectives by feminists of color.* San Franscisco: Aunt Lute Books.

Collins, P. (1990). *Black feminist thought: Knowledge, consciousness, and the politics of empowerment.* New York: Routledge.

Collins, P. (1995). The social construction of Black feminist thought. In B. Guy-Sheftall (Ed.), *Words of fire: An anthology of African-American feminist thought* (pp. 338–357). New York: The New Press.

Etter-Lewis, G. (1993). *My soul is my own: Oral narratives of African American women in the professions.* New York: Routledge.

Freire, P. (1970). *Pedagogy of the oppressed.* New York: Routledge.

Hine, D., & Thompson, K. (1998). *A shining thread of hope: The history of Black women in America.* New York: Broadway Books.

Hooks, B. (1994). *Teaching to transgress.* New York: Routledge.

Gitlin, A. (Ed.). (1994). *Power and method: Political activism and educational research.* New York: Routledge.

Gramsci, A. (1971). *Selections from the Prison Notebooks.* New York: International Publishers Co.

Guy-Sheftall, B. (Ed.). (1995). *Words of fire: An anthology of African-American feminist thought.* New York: The New Press.

Ladson-Billings, G. (1994). *The dreamkeepers: Successful teachers of African American children.* San Francisco: Jossey-Bass.

Lemert, C., & Bhan, E. (Eds.). (1998). *The voice of Anna Julia Cooper.* Lanham, MD: Rowman & Littlefield.

Lorde, A. (1995). Age, race, class, and sex: Women redefining difference. In B. Guy-Sheftall (Ed.), *Words of fire: An anthology of African-American feminist thought,* (pp. 284–291). New York: The New Press.

Morrison, T. (1992). *Playing in the dark: Whiteness and the literary imagination.* Cambridge, MA: Harvard University Press.

Reyes, M. de la Luz. (1992). Challenging venerable assumptions: Literacy instruction for linguistically different students. *Harvard Educational Review, 62*(4), 427–446.

Spina, S., & Tai, R. (1998). *The politics of racial identity: A pedagogy of invisibility.* [Book Review]. *Educational Researcher, 27*(1), 36–40, 48.

Stanfield, J. (1994). Ethnic modeling in qualitative research. In N. Denzin & Y. Lincoln (Eds.), *Handbook of qualitative research.* Newbury Park, CA: Sage.

Willis, A. (1995). Reading the world: Contextualizing the school literacy experiences of a young African-American male. *Harvard Educational Review, 65*(1), 30–49.

5

Looking Two Ways: Identity, Research, and Praxis in the Caribbean Community

Annette Henry
University of Illinois-Chicago

LOCATING MYSELF

In this personal story, I want to discuss my identity, research methodology, and practice as I work with African Caribbean teachers, parents, and students. I was born in England, of Jamaican parents. I grew up in the UK and moved to Canada in 1965. I have lived in the United States since 1992. I have been a classroom teacher as well as a teacher of secondary and university students. On my mother's side, I come from a family many of whose members, particularly in England, have practiced a social gospel, one in which engaged spiritual practice involved seeking educational, social, and economic justice for the Caribbean community. As a child, I learned about the interconnections between spirituality, praxis, and social justice. As an adult, I learned more about these creative connections from Black womanists and feminists (e.g., Ani, 1994; Cannon, 1995; Cliff, 1986; hooks, 1994; James, 1993; Sanders, 1995; Townes, 1995). My various life stories and geographies, then, have contributed to conceptual framework, my research questions and approaches.

I am a Black feminist.[1] Feminism, by definition, is concerned with social change. It has been suggested that all feminist research can be considered action research because of this social change agenda (Reinharz, 1992). Being a Black feminist raises questions: Who am I? How does who I am affect my work? How do I define my work? How does my background help/hinder my relationships with community participants? Whose standards and meanings do I use in my research? To understand my commitments to Black feminism and working in the African Caribbean community, I shall share some autobiographical details.

I came to the study of African Caribbean Canadian women teachers' epistemology and practice in graduate school in Toronto. I arrived at this political passion when I soon realized that Black women's voices were missing from educational discourses. Although a few American scholars (e.g., Foster, Ladson-Billings, King, etc.) had been working on the practices of Black teachers, educational literature, for the most part, continued to disqualify these teachers' knowledge and practice. Moreover, normative, Eurocentric, patriarchal biases continued to perpetuate pejorative discourses on the pathological Black family—deviant (absent) father, overly strong mother—as well as a discourse of Black student underachievement.

Since 1989, I have been doing research that examines the lives and teaching practices of Black women teachers and, more recently, that examines the learning of young adolescent Black girls. Although I am working in an African American setting, most of my research, both in Canada and the United States has been with members of the Caribbean community. My own life history, then, has influenced my conceptual framework for examining the contradictions and complexities of African Caribbean teachers who strive to forge alternative practices for their students in the United States and Canada. I seek to investigate the possibilities of Black teachers' cultural knowledge to transform education. I seek to explore pedagogical issues from alternative cultural standpoints, that is, from the social reality of less powerful members of society.

This is an exciting time in research. Scholars from "marginalized groups" are conducting research from their own standpoints. Although my epistemic viewpoint acknowledges the importance of academic research, I want to underscore that one must be leery of unproblematized cultural standpoints and insider/outsider dichotomies (Stanfield, 1994), as well as of essentialized and monolithic views about Black females (Mama, 1995). I also want to empha-

---

[1]Barbara Omolade (1994) explains: "Black feminism is sometimes referred to as *womanism* because both are concerned with the struggles against sexism and racism by Black women who are themselves part of the community's efforts to achieve equity and liberty"(p. xx). A choice of one term over another, regardless of overlapping meanings, reminds us of the complexity and diversities of positionalities, as well as their political implications.

size that the cultural standpoints of Black people have been suppressed by the dominant groups. Our histories have often been "written by strangers, who have sojourned among us but who have little knowledge of us" (Okihiro, 1984, p. 208).

I certainly am not negating some of the important work done by White scholars. One well-known example is Gerda Lerner (1973), who has done groundbreaking historical writing on Black women in America. However, as Alice Walker (1983) explains, "the truth about any subject only comes when all the sides of the story are put together and these different meanings make one new one" (p. 49).

Educational and sociological theory need critical, nonessentialist discourses about Black women and girls in the African diaspora. Cross-cultural research is one way to contribute to this project. Cultures may be connected, at the same time revealing diversities and complexities.

In this chapter, I talk about my work in the Caribbean community in Illinois. I have been working with Enid Johnson (a pseudonym) and her immigrant female students from the Caribbean since 1995. The cross-cultural component to my work contributes to the nonessentialized views I mentioned earlier. Black women scholars have argued for more empirical and cross-cultural investigations of the life experiences of women (James, 1993; Scott, 1977). Indeed, Shulamit Reinharz (1992) writes: "Cross-cultural awareness is not particularly high among U.S. feminists" (p. 116). The importance of cross-cultural/cross-national work can illustrate the interconnections and dissimilarities in the African Caribbean diaspora. I theorize about the lives and knowledge of Black women and girls by analyzing the commonalities and differences of Black experiences across various learning contexts. This agenda will enable me to identify new questions and starting points with which to broaden my own praxis.

METHODOLOGY: CONCEPTUAL DECOLONIZATION

The dominant culture teaches us to privilege some ways of knowing and devalue others. Kwasi Wiredu (1996) argues for the necessity of "conceptual decolonization," claiming that the language of institutional education forces us to think outside of our indigenous ways of knowing, thinking, and speaking. Many Black women scholars have critiqued the imperialism in sociological and educational research, opening up relationships of participation, collaboration, and dialogue; they have theorized power and empowerment in innovative ways, as well as forged alternative methodologies (e.g., Ani, 1994; Cannon, 1995; Cliff, 1986; hooks, 1994; James, 1993; King & Mitchell, 1995; Lorde, 1984; Sanders, 1995; Townes, 1995). For example, striving for a more holistic approach in the Black community, Joyce

King and Carolyn Ann Mitchell (1995) developed a methodology relevant to the lives of Black women which involved group conversation. My commitment to feminist research critiques these imperialist methods and power relationships inherent in much social science research regarding Black women and girls. (See Henry, 1995 for a review of the portrayal of Black girls in the research literature.) I agree with Stanfield (1994) that we have to "allow the examined people of color to articulate holistic explanations about how they construct their realities" (p. 185).

INTERSUBJECTIVITY AND SOCIAL RELATIONS

I acknowledge that I may consciously or unconsciously tap into various elements of my background as I conduct my research and work with participants. Certain dimensions of my personal history may bring certain intersubjective understandings into the research moment, as well as, perhaps, engender certain blind spots. Each researcher is part of a collective historicocultural memory in the social world that she investigates (Darroch & Silvers, 1982). At this postmodern moment, many terms are under debate and review, e.g.: "Black," "community," "subjectivity." Researchers are reminding us that we are a constellation of multiple, hybrid identities; these subjectivities may render our own and our participants' cultural constructions problematic. In "Feminist Insider Dilemmas," for example, Patricia Zavella (1997) describes some of the dilemmas faced when studying Chicana working mothers; that is, the researcher shared the same ethnicity, class, and gender as her respondents. Her own understandings of Chicana feminist identity hindered the participants' constructions of themselves.

One cannot unproblematically assume commonality on the basis of class, culture, gender, or any other socio-historico-political dimensions. Yet, certain commonalities in cultural background with my participants has facilitated aspects of my research. For example: February 14, 1995—my first meeting with Enid Johnson. During the first few minutes of introducing myself, I was gently and cautiously explaining my prior research. She interrupted:

> E.J.:   Tell you what....
> A.H.:   Uh huh?
> E.J.:   Come to my class whenever you feel like....
> A.H.:   Oh ...
> E.J.:   And I'll tell the children.
> A.H.:   All right.
> E.J.:   I'll do anything to help you. You are part of me.
> A.H.:   I appreciate that.
> E.J.:   I definitely will. Come to my class anytime and do your observation, and who knows where you'll go from there?

Overcome, tears filled my eyes. Then I breathed easily. Access can take up to a year to negotiate (see Hammersley & Atkinson, 1995). Despite our complex and variegated backgrounds, Enid perceived me as "part of her." Thus, the negotiations regarding gaining entry were bypassed. I do not want to portray romantically that working in such "minority contexts" is without problems or dilemmas. Interviews with Caribbean working-class mothers have helped me rethink my praxis, that is, "the effort to remake and transcend" (Greene, 1994, p. 24). Race and gender are not enough to abate tensions created by power relationships between researchers and participants. I became uncomfortably aware of the ways in which our class and education were constructed through language. Which language? Whose language? These were questions that had to be "negotiated" on the spot, almost intuitively. Adele, a Jamaican, just blasted through the interview in full gear, seeming not to mind whether or not I understood her "patois," but assuming I did. Marie-France, a Haitian mother, often hesitated in her interview, asking for clarification of my questions. I also suffered from conversational insecurity, wondering whether we should speak in French (which carries its own set of ideological framings), wondering whether she might feel that her English was not good enough if I initiated a language switch. These father tongues, rather than mother tongues (Creoles), remind us, in some sense, of what Davies (1995) calls "the master discourse," a language that categorizes and positions us all in a "polyphonic discourse" that is, a "discourse that reflects the realities of those who must speak through more than one language/culture at once" (Chancy, 1997, p. 11).

As a researcher in this working-class community where missing work means not being paid, I have learned to be flexible regarding the availability of participants for interviews. We have had difficulty finding convenient times with respect to mothers' work schedules. In fact, I have let go of some of my researcher aspirations and ambitions as a way to show respect for the demands of their everyday lives.

I have been working with Enid and her students since 1995, developing two different projects. It was Enid's invitation to work with the girls and help them to "open up," and express themselves, that led me to develop an ongoing reading/writing/discussion group with her students. My inquiries in this context have caused me to think about the expectations, demands, and attitudes of participants regarding research and the researcher. Indeed, I aim to be "accountable, " "useful," "reflexive" and "reciprocal" in the relationship.

I am mindful of my commitments and purpose of working in the Black community as a Black female researcher, thus, I do not want to participate in "hit-and-run" research, as Kirin Narayan (1997) explains, research "in which engagement with vibrant individuals is flattened by the demands of a scholarly career" (p. 30). Reflexivity, usefulness, and accountability may take on many forms. For example, I have occasionally given talks at the local African Caribbean church where Enid and many of her students are members. This site is also a rich place for understanding her epistemology and practice in her classroom. As Stanfield (1994) argues, "many Afro-Americans and other people of color (especially aboriginal populations) cannot be understood fully unless the central place of spirituality in their lives is given serious consideration" (p. 185). Usefulness has sometimes meant helping various community members.

Relationships are hard work and take time. My ongoing relationship with participants in this setting has precipitated an action-oriented relationship. For instance, my literacy program with Caribbean American girls is a form of commitment to social change, a project that aims to help Black girls socially, intellectually, academically, and culturally. I have described this project elsewhere as "outsearch" (see Henry, 1998), as a way of exploding the academic polarity of theory (research /practice (outreach).

Because research has been a historical act of domination against Black people, I aim, through my research, to be reflexive, vulnerable, and dialogic. I aim to respect and incorporate the ideas and thoughts of participants in the methodology; I aim to be accessible in all stages of the research process. For example, although I indeed develop a design and methodology, I confer with participants regarding concerns, observations, findings, and pressing concerns from their points of view. Their input shapes the boundaries and the design. Sometimes being accessible and vulnerable involves engaging in difficult conversations about what is happening in the teaching/learning process.

As the following example of the researcher–participant relationship illustrates, in my relationship with the classroom teacher Enid, we supported each other and worked in tandem, our ideas sometimes cross-fertilizing each other's: The girls in my research study in 1996–1997 often ate lunch with Enid in her classroom. One day in April, during their lunch hour, I introduced a photo-essay activity, in which each girl was given a disposable camera; they were asked to decide how they were going to create their photomontage (e.g., scrapbook with written explanations). We sat and planned out how they were going to go about the project (e.g., using the camera, taking photos, keeping track of photos taken before developing them,timelines, and creating a life-story book). While she was organizing materials in another part of the room, Enid overheard. She jumped in, helping me explain the activity with concepts and expressions that she was using in her teaching and which were helpful to the girls: "graphic organizer" "road map" "Why do I want to...." "What if...." After the children left, we brainstormed about different ways that this exercise could be used and expanded on in Enid's teaching, and the many cognitive, language, and social skills that it could help develop.

ON BIASES AND BACKGROUNDS

This *is* an exciting time in educational research. New epistemologies have emerged from previously silenced groups. The concept of the "aloof researcher" is often abandoned; more action-oriented, activist-oriented research is emerging. Grand narratives are being replaced by local, small-scale theories fitted to specific problems and situations. Heretofore neglected groups/topics are being researched in new ways, foregrounding dimensions such as culture, race, gender, sexuality, language, and religion (Denzin 1997; Lather, 1994; Reinharz, 1992). Despite this, however, the hegemony of traditional, positivistic research prevails. A Black female researcher conducting research with Black women and girls is easily accused of "bias." For example, an anonymous reviewer from a professional journal wrote: "It is always difficult if you declare your value position as a feminist. [You choose] … empirical findings to prove one's value position."

Indeed, researchers have predispositions. There seems to be a presumption that in a "valid," "reliable" study, the researcher remains objective, detached, disembodied, and without bias, defined as "blind spots that serve to distort data" according to a conventional textbook on educational research (Charles, 1998, p. 362). As I mentioned earlier, in reality, research has been very biased against, even deceptive regarding Black people. One recent example is *The Bell Curve* (Herrenstein & Murray, 1994). Indeed, bias can indicate a "predisposition or prejudice, an inclination, leaning or bent." (*Oxford English Dictionary*). The notion of bias also carries a historical meaning of "looking two ways." I appropriate this Januslike position of bringing my biases and inclinations up front. I recognize that my North American experiences and training and my cultural ways of knowing help me serve both the research community and the African Caribbean community. These biases or inclinations, personal history, and identity have given me insights into my work, into my research environment. They help shape and reshape my praxis. I also realize I have much to learn.

REFERENCES

Ani, M. (1994). *Yurugu: An African-centered critique of European Cultural thought and behavior.* Trenton, NJ: Africa World Press.

Atkinson, P. (1981). *The clinical experience.* Farnborough: Gower.

Cannon, K. (1995). *Katie's cannon: Womanism and the soul of the Black community.* New York: Continuum.

Chancy, M. (1997). *Framing silence: Revolutionary novels by Haitian women.* New York: Routledge.

Charles, C. (1998). *Introduction to educational research.* (3rd ed). New York: Addison Wesley Longman.

Cliff, M. (1986). "I found god in myself and I loved her/I loved her fiercely": More thoughts on the work of Black women artists. *Journal of feminist studies in religion 2* (1), 7–39.

Darroch, V. & R. Silvers. (1982). Biography and Discourse. In *Interpretive human studies* (pp. 3–21). Washington: University Press of America.

Davies, C. (1995). Hearing Black women's voices: Transgressing imposed boundaries. In C. Boyce Davies & 'M. Ogundipe-Leslie (Eds.), *Moving beyond boundaries,* Vol.1. New York: New York University Press.

Denzin, N. (1997). *Interpretive ethnography.* Thousand Oaks, CA: Sage.

Greene, M. (1994). The lived world. In L. Stone (Ed.), *The education feminism reader* (pp. 17–25). New York: Routledge.

Hammersley, M. & Atkinson, P. (1995). *Ethnography.* New York: Routledge.

Henry, A. (1995). Growing up Black, female and working class: A teacher's narrative, *Anthropology and Education Quarterly, 26* (3), 279–305.

Herrnstein, R. & Murray, C. (1994). *The bell curve: Intelligence and class structure in American Life.* New York: Free Press.

hooks, b. (1994). *Teaching to transgress.* New York: Routledge.

James, J. (1993). Reflections on teaching: "Gender, race, and class." *Feminist teacher, 5* (3), 9–15.

King, J., & Mitchell, C. (1995). *Black mothers to sons.* New York: Peter Lang.

Lather, P. (1994). *Troubling the angels.* New York: Routledge.

Lerner, G. (1973) *Black women in White America: A documentary history.* New York: Oxford University Press.

Lorde, A. (1984). *Sister outsider.* New York: The Crossing Press.

Mama, A. (1995). *Beyond the masks* London. Routledge.

Narayan, K. (1997). How native is a native anthropologist? In L. Lamphere, H. Ragoné, & P. Zavella (Eds.), *Situated lives* (pp. 23–41). New York: Routledge.

Okihiro, G. (1984). "The writing of ethnic history." In D. Dunaway & W. Baum (Eds.), *Oral history and interdisciplinary anthology* (pp. 195–211). Nashville, TN: The American Association for State and Local History in cooperation with the Oral History Association.

Omolade, B. (1994). *The rising song of African American women.* New York: Routledge.

Reinharz, S. (1992). *Feminist methods in social science research.* New York: Oxford University Press.

Sanders, C. (1995). *Living at the intersection: Womanism and Afrocentrism in theology.* Minneapolis, MN: Augsburg Fortress.

Scott, P. B. (1977). Debunking Sapphire: Toward a non-sexist and non-racist social science. *Journal of Sociology and Social Welfare, 4,* 864–871.

Stanfield, J. (1994). Ethnic modeling in qualitative research.In N. Denzin & Y. Lincoln (Eds.), *Handbook of qualitative research* (pp. 175–188). Newbury Park, CA: Sage.

Townes, E. (1995). *In a blaze of glory: Womanist spirituality as social witness.* Nashville, TN: Abingdon.

Walker, A. (1983). In search of our mother's gardens. San Diego, CA: Harcourt Brace Jovanovich.

Zavella, P. (1997). Feminist insider dilemmas. In L. Lamphere, H. Ragoné, & P. Zavella, (Eds.). *Situated lives* (pp. 42–61). New York: Routledge.

6

Research or Personal Quest? Dilemmas in Studying My Own Kind

Beloo Mehra
University of Illinois at Urbana-Champaign

Interactions between researcher and respondents cannot be removed from the research equation, even if one wishes to do so. The presence of such interactions can be treated as an opportunity to be exploited, and as a means to get to a better understanding of the nature of reality as constructed by the respondents and the researcher. The concept of the active observer "researching out and touching, to try ideas to see if they worked," is entirely consistent with the positivist point of view (Lincoln & Guba, 1985, p. 92). The general belief in the advantageous effect of separating investigator and object, in the positivist tradition, is based on the premise of subject–object dualism, the investigator being the subject and the entity under study being the object (Lincoln & Guba, 1985). The naturalistic researcher, however, believes that the inquirer and the object of inquiry interact to influence one another, and that the knower and known are inseparable.

The situation is more compelling in case of human research, which is inherently dialectical. If a researcher seeks to understand human experience, he or she must be in a constant, sensitive, and dialogical relationship with other humans. Also, the researcher must be able to deal with the conflicts and contradictions that emerge through an interplay of various oppositional forces of the respondents' realities and his or her own reality. Thus, the researcher, in the naturalistic paradigm of inquiry, is not just an observer; he or she both disturbs the research setting and is also disturbed by it. It is in this

69

framework of a "disturbing and disturbed observer" (Lincoln and Guba, 1985, p. 92), that I pen down following thoughts.

An important dimension to doing naturalistic research is the perspective that the researcher brings to the research setting—including his or her bias and subjectivity. In studying the experiences of people from a particular ethnic group, the case becomes more intriguing when the researcher belongs to the same ethnic group as the respondents. In this chapter, I describe my experiences as an Asian Indian woman researcher conducting a study of Asian Indian families and children (Mehra, 1996). I explore the ways in which my identity interacted with that of research participants and the research setting. I also elucidate the manner in which my bias and subjectivity shaped my study and its findings.

The chapter is divided into four sections. In the first section, I explore some methodological issues that emerged as a result of the interactions between my identities and those of my research participants. The second section deals with the dilemma of being a researcher or an advocate; the third describes the dilemma of being a researcher or a friend. In the final section, I ponder on an enigma of a personal nature, which I believe other researchers should contemplate also during their own research. This section asks the most basic questions: Why do a study? What significance does it have for me as an individual, and not just as a researcher? The ordering of the sections is in no way an indicator of their relative significance or value.

POSITIONALITY OF THE RESEARCHER
AND METHODOLOGICAL CONCERNS

"Interpretive research begins and ends with the biography and self of the researcher."
—Denzin (1989, p. 12)

Anthropologist Nita Kumar has published her memoirs of doing fieldwork in a city of cultural and historic significance in India, in her book entitled *Friends, Brothers, and Informants: Fieldwork Memoirs of Banaras* (1992). She has given a compelling narrative of encounters between her "Self," as "an Indian doing research in India, an Indian—though based abroad and at home abroad—by birth, nationality and choice" (p. 11), and the "Other," the people of Banaras whom she studied. Kumar argues that an indigene studying his or her own society is engaged not only in a more activist project, and in more of a voyage of self-discovery, but also in a more holistic project, one that is more generous in its methodological approaches and more liberal in its scope. Thus, it seems appropriate to start with discussing some of the key methodological concerns that emerged from my research with

Asian Indians in the United States, and the encounters that I, as an Asian Indian researcher, have had with my respondents.

Knowing Myself and My Research Interests

Krieger (1991) wrote that "we ought to acknowledge, more honestly than we do, the extent to which our studies are reflections of our inner lives." (p. 1). I am an international doctoral student from India, and am currently working on my dissertation research to study the educational experiences of children of Asian Indian immigrant families as mediated by the relations between their parents and schools. I am using a selected sample of Asian Indian immigrant families (people of Indian origin, who migrated from India) to illustrate the general phenomenon of the cultural model of schooling and its working in minority families. By applying the concept of cultural model to understand the role of parental involvement in the education of children in selected Asian Indian immigrant families, I am working at an intersecting standpoint of home–school relationship and minority education.

Taking a step backward here, I now want to inform readers why I decided to study this topic and what my past and present experiences had to do with the selection of my research topic. In other words, I find it important to reflect on the influence of my identity as a researcher on the choice of my research area. Scheurich (1994) remarks that one's historical position, one's class (which may or may not include changes over the course of a lifetime), one's race, one's gender, one's region, one's religion, and so on— all of these interact and influence, limit and constrain production of knowledge (Scheurich, 1994). I was a high school teacher in India for 5 years before I came to the United States and started my doctoral program. During my first year and a half in graduate school, I was actively involved with a local cultural organization that organized social and cultural gatherings for the Asian Indian population in the town. Once a week, I also volunteered to help an Asian Indian couple in their Sunday home school where they gave native language instruction to a group of children from Asian Indian immigrant families. These direct and frequent contacts with immigrant families and their children forced me to reflect on my experiences as an international student trying to adjust and adapt in a new educational and cultural environment. The nature of my research assistantships during 2 years of my graduate work was also instrumental in significant ways. I was involved in two research projects that dealt with the educational experiences and achievement of Mexican immigrant teenagers in high school. While researching the literature on Mexican immigrants, I became interested in systematically exploring the literature on immigrants from India. I found that although there was some research on the acculturation and adaptation of immigrants from India, not much had been said about the educational experiences and performance of children of these immigrants.

A preliminary review of the literature and my perception of the need for more research in the area of immigrant education, and specifically the education of Asian Indian immigrants, combined with the driving force of my identity as Asian Indian, led me to concentrate my focus on Asian Indian immigrant families. I also believe that my present position as a doctoral student in the field of education (as opposed to any other field, like economics), which was my major as an undergraduate and for my Masters degree) played an important role in the selection of my research area. The issues of education of minority children in American schools, to which I was exposed in my courses and through my research assistantships, undoubtedly influenced my decision. This aspect of my evolving self as a researcher is more a matter of my deliberate choice and cognitive reasoning, in contrast to my historical and social position grounded in my ethnicity. I now believe that the first and foremost area where a researcher's self influences his or her research is in the selection of a research topic. Who I am determines, to a large extent, what I want to study.

In order to narrow down my research interests to a manageable dissertation problem, I decided to conduct a pilot study to explore the various general aspects of the education of Asian Indian children in American schools. This pilot, or as I prefer to call it, predissertation study portrayed the educational experiences of four Asian Indian children in a multicultural elementary school (Mehra, 1996). I attempted to narrate the stories of these children from their perspective as well as from their parents' and teachers' perspectives. The data was collected over the period of a school semester, through classroom observations, and semistructured and open interviews with the children, their parents, teachers, and the school principal. The study provided an insight into some of the conflicts and pressures children in the immigrant minorities face as they struggle with the duality of their cultural and social experiences. It also helped me to understand the place of schooling in an immigrant minority group's experiences and belief system. The findings suggested important linkages between the families and schools of these children. Studying these homeschool connections in Asian Indian families became my dissertation research topic.

As I progressed with my predissertation study—planning, collecting, and analyzing data, and writing the results—I was constantly attentive to the emerging conflicts between my Asian Indian identity and my role as a researcher. I kept a journal to record some of these conflicts and dilemmas, which became the foundation for this chapter.

Researcher's Identity: Outsider–Insider Perspective

I have been living in the United States for more than 4 years now with my husband, who is also a doctoral student. Being an Asian Indian does make me an insider in many ways to the culture and ways of life of my Asian Indian research participants, giving me an advantage in understanding their perspectives. I could identify with some of the beliefs of the parents who participated in my study. I was able to understand their reasons for many of their opinions and behaviors, like preferring to eat Indian food and wearing Indian dresses on weekends or while at home because it made them feel "at home." I was also tempted to reflect on some of my own frequent behaviors, like checking out Indian books and magazines at the Asian Library in the university or renting videos of Hindi films over the weekends, in addition to the behaviors mentioned by my respondents. Like the parents in my study, I also try to keep in touch with my ethnic identity by seeking out the company of other Asian Indians and by speaking in my native language with them. This latter aspect was also reflected in the language that was most often used for parent interviews. I gave parents the choice of talking either in Hindi or English, whichever they felt comfortable in, and most of them chose Hindi. This in itself indicated their desire to maintain their Asian Indian identity, which they also emphasized for their children. As an insider, I found it easy to understand why these parents were so keen that their children should maintain their Indian identity, and not become totally "Americanized."

I was also an outsider to the research setting in two important ways. First, I do not have any children and have not personally experienced some of the dilemmas Asian Indian parents may face in regard to bringing up their children in a cultural setting much different from the one they grew up in. Based on my casual conversations with some Asian Indian and other international friends who had children, I had some perspective on these conflicts. Although not having experienced these issues myself, conducting this research gave me an opportunity to understand in depth the reactions of these parents when they see their children getting "Americanized." I also learned their reasons for emphasizing the use of their native language at home. Some of my personal beliefs about issues related to maintaining the native language and culture in immigrant families were also challenged by some of the findings of the study. Based on my increased understanding of the interactions between children's experiences at home and at school, and their struggles with their bicultural identities, my perspective on these issues has now become more child oriented than it was before I did the study.

I was also an outsider to the American public school system, which was an important part of this study. I was not aware of many of the policies in regard to the minority and limited English proficient (LEP) children in schools, the multicultural programs to support these children, and the role of district, state, and federal government in financing these programs. These issues came up frequently in my conversations with the school principal and teachers, and became important factors in understanding the children's experiences at school. Being an outsider in the school gave me an opportunity to understand these important aspects of school-level policies and practices from the perspectives of teachers and the principal. In some ways, my identity as an international student was nonthreatening to most of the teachers in the school, and they felt quite comfortable in giving me access to their classrooms and offices. My lack of knowledge about the American school system enabled me to ask the most basic questions and probe the school personnel for details in order to get their viewpoints on many school and classroom issues. I found teachers and principals very supportive of my study; and in many instances they went to great lengths to make sure that I understood what they were saying. Being an outsider helped me to be more attentive, reflective, and critical of what I observed in children's classrooms.

Notion of Reality and the Objective–Subjective Debate

Closely related to the issue of insider–outsider dichotomy is the issue of objective–subjective reality in research. The researchers working in the naturalistic paradigm believe that there is no single, objective reality "out there," and that people perceive and construct their own realities based on their experiences and understanding of the world around them (Lincoln & Guba, 1985). Qualitative researchers attempt to capture the world of their research participants by understanding their perceived realities and interpreting them from their own subjective perspectives as researchers and individuals. Krieger (1991) believes that the outer world, or our "external reality" is inseparable from what we already know based on our lives and experiences—our inner reality. In fact, she argues that the knowledge of the external world is only a small part of what our total knowledge can be; what we ever really know is, in essence, self. Thus, the reality that we all see is based on our understanding of the world, which in turn is based on our knowledge of the self. To use Scheurich's (1994) phrase; "How I see shapes, frames, determines, and even creates what I see" (p. 17).

Since the objective of my predissertation study was to understand the experiences of Asian Indian children and their families, it became clear to me that the reality I was seeking was constructed in nature. I was trying to make sense of people's subjective experiences and their constructions of those experiences. They were telling me their feelings and opinions about certain things or certain aspects of their lives, and I was attempting to understand how they made sense of their experiences. In other words, I was making sense of their sense of reality. In this way, I was actually constructing reality, based on the constructions of reality of my participants. My subjective and constructed realities and those of my research participants, and the interactions among these various realities were thus the foundation for this study.

Even though the primary objective of the study was to understand the experiences of the children, I found it important to understand their parents' perceptions of the children's educational experiences, and also to get a sense of the teachers' experiences with Asian Indian children. Thus, I was working with multiple realities, or sometimes multiple constructions of a single reality. As an example, the regular classroom teacher identified Veena, one of the children in the study, as a shy girl. Veena also identified herself as shy, but only in some specific situations, like in the regular classroom when she had to work in a group with some American students and because she was not able to understand some of the words other children in the group used. Veena's ESL (English as a Second Language) teacher, when talking about Veena's interactions or behavior in the classroom, did not refer to her as shy, but as well disciplined. Was it because in the ESL classroom Veena was often a more active participant in various activities, as compared to her behavior in her regular classroom, that her ESL teacher did not see her as shy? What was present in the ESL classroom or was missing from the regular classroom that made Veena behave and feel in certain ways? There was no single objective reality that could help answer these questions.

Researcher as Instrument: Data Collection and Analysis

For primary data gathering in a naturalistic inquiry, it would be virtually impossible to devise an a priori nonhuman instrument with sufficient adaptability to encompass and adjust to the variety of realities that are encountered. Lincoln & Guba (1985) argue that only a human instrument is capable of grasping and evaluating the meanings of various interactions that take place between the researcher and the respondents. They further claim that because all instruments are value based, only a human instrument is in a position to identify and take into account, to some extent, the resulting biases. In my predissertation study also, certain methodological tensions emerged as a result of my role as the primary instrument for collecting and analyzing data.

An important aspect of data collection in my study was the "You know how it is!" pattern. Parents in the study often assumed that my being an Asian Indian enabled me to understand their viewpoint completely and thoroughly. In order not to make any hasty judgments or interpretations on my part, I had to be persistent but polite in asking them what they thought about various issues. I often found myself saying to them, "I am afraid I don't know how it is, could you please say more about what you mean." This, by no means, suggested that I ignored my personal worldview and my understanding of life as an Asian Indian; it simply reinforced my determination to understand the realities of my research participants and their perspectives on living and raising children in the United States.

Language appeared as another important issue during data collection. As mentioned earlier, I conducted many of the parent interviews in Hindi; these were later translated into English during transcribing. Translation sometimes posed as a problem because, as in any language, some of the expressions and exclamations in Hindi were not directly translatable into English, and I was concerned about losing the essence of the parents' views. The language issue occasionally entered the classrooms as well, where I was conducting observations. In one particular instance, I had mixed feelings of happiness, surprise, and discomfort when one of the Asian Indian children in the kindergarten started talking to me in Hindi in the classroom. I was not sure whether to continue talking to him in Hindi or start talking in English, given the class setting and presence of other students.

Another concern during data collection was the presentation of myself as a researcher. When I went to interview Asian Indian families in their homes, I was not sure how to dress—Indian or otherwise. I was not certain of the kinds of messages I would be sending to the parents and children if I wore a traditional Indian dress, or if I wore a casual American outfit. Should I present myself as a researcher or as an Asian Indian researcher, or just as an Asian Indian woman to these families? The issue was further complicated by my regular visits to children's classrooms, where they saw me in somewhat more professional American attire, which seemed appropriate for the school.

At many points in the study I had to struggle with my own bias creeping into the data collection and analysis. For example, I was a little surprised to find the absence of any Indian artifact and keepsake at the Devens's home (one of the families in the study). To me, some of my Indian possessions make me feel so much at home, and continually remind me of my identity. But I realize now that it may not matter as much to many Asian Indians to have their homes "look Indian" as it means to me.

The data analysis in the study was more holistic in nature, as I was trying to paint a comprehensive picture of the experiences of these children and the ways in which their being Asian Indian shaped their experiences at school. I was using a wide-angle lens to understand these children's experiences at school, rather than confining the experiences to their specific classrooms. In other words, I was more interested in the general patterns emerging from the data than the individual teacher-level or class-level factors that could or could not facilitate the children's adjustment at school. However, there were instances when I was fighting my urge to evaluate the individual teaching styles and behaviors of the teachers in the classes that I observed. Occasionally I was caught in a conflict between my role as a researcher and as an advocate for Asian Indian children in those classrooms. The next section deals with this issue in detail.

THE DETACHED OBSERVER: RESEARCH–ADVOCACY DILEMMA

Recently, advocacy approaches to research, which are openly valuebased, have added their voices to the present methodological ferment in empirical research in education. Researchers working in the "emancipatory" paradigms, such as critical, neo-Marxist, feminist, race-specific, praxis-oriented, and participatory paradigms, consider overtly value-based advocacy research—which is openly opposed to the maldistribution of power—as neither more nor less ideological than the mainstream research (Lather, 1992). Rather, those committed to research approaches that challenge the status quo and contribute to a more egalitarian social order are considered to have made an epistemological break from the positivist insistence on researcher neutrality and objectivity. The increasing emphasis on advocacy paradigms in educational research is permeating the boundaries of naturalistic research, which is generally conducted in order to understand human experience and to interpret the perceived realities of research participants. Some of the issues that I faced in my predissertation study, and will also encounter in my dissertation study, are linked with this notion of advocacy research versus research for understanding.

There were times in my study when I found myself on the verge of defending Asian Indian parents and certain of their behaviors. One such instance occurred when some teachers told me that Asian Indian parents did not generally involve themselves in the school. These parents' involvement in their children's education ended outside the school gates, and its manifestation in the form of volunteering at the school or attending PTA events was totally absent. When the teachers and principal told me about the lack of parents' direct involvement in the school, my first impulse was to say something in defense of these parents. I immediately thought of many reasons why they did not or could not volunteer—for example, their busy schedules, lack of knowledge of the English language, and unfamiliarity with the American school system, and so on. Although all of these reasons seemed appropriate, and some of the teachers also appeared to be aware of them, I decided not to say anything on behalf of my research participants and simply try to understand the teachers' perspectives.

I also struggled with my role as a researcher and as an advocate for Asian Indian children in the school. I was disturbed to find the lack of native language support these children had in a school that had a well-recognized and established "multicultural program." The multicultural program and policies of this school played an important role in the maintenance of native language and culture of these children. The school emphasized the need for using the native language at home, not only for casual conversations but also for discussing academic concepts in order to facilitate the expansion of the children's vocabulary in their native language. In addition, the school provided instruction in about 15 different languages to native speakers for a period of 35 to 40 minutes a day. There were some policy restrictions to this, however, which applied to Asian Indian students in the school as well. With respect to the policy and the financial constraints associated with that policy, the school had to have at least five Asian Indian students who spoke the same Indian language in order to provide instruction in that language. But among the total number of Asian Indian students at the school, only a few were native Hindi speakers, another few were native Kannada speakers, and yet another few were native Gujarati speakers. In other words, there was not a large enough group of students who had a common native Indian language. As a result, the school could not offer native language support in any Indian language the way it did for the Chinese or the Korean students.

In my interviews with Asian Indian parents and children (not only those participating in my study, but also other Asian Indian families whose children attended the same school or other schools in the district), I found that parents wanted some kind of native language instruction at the school. Most of the children also expressed willingness and enthusiasm to learn their language at school. This expectation, especially from the families whose children attended the particular school in the study, may have been mainly because of their awareness of the school's multicultural program, and the services available for native language instruction for other language groups in the school. However, more important was the fact that even though many families had a mother tongue other than Hindi (the most commonly spoken Indian language, especially in the north and central regions of India), the parents wanted instruction in Hindi at school. Some of them reasoned, "It is better to have something rather than nothing." Thus, though the school did not have a large enough number of Asian Indian children who spoke the same Indian language in order to arrange for instruction in that language, it could offer native language support in Hindi, which was welcomed, and in fact demanded by, the parents. As an advocate for Asian Indian parents and children, I brought this fact to the attention of the administrator of the multicultural program. I also offered to volunteer in the school to teach Hindi to Asian Indian children in the school; but due to scheduling problems, that arrangement could not be finalized.

This discussion raises an important issue: How rational is it to be an advocate for the people you are studying? And, more importantly, how rational a choice will it be for me as a beginner in the world of academics to enter the field of advocacy research? As an international doctoral student who has yet to complete her dissertation, will it be sensible for me to become an advocate for the population that I will work with, and specifically the population that I belong to and care for? If I knew the answers to these questions, I would not have written this chapter! But the merit of these questions lies not in the knowledge of their answers, but in their ability to provide researchers with yet another tool to reflect on their research methodology.

FELLOW NATIVES AND INFORMANTS: RESEARCHER–FRIEND DILEMMA

Denzin (1989) argues that because the goal of interpretive interactionism (a framework resulting from a combination of symbolic interactionism and other traditions, such as naturalistic inquiry, and case study approach) is to connect the researched's world of lived experiences and the world of the reader, one of the ways that that can most effectively be accomplished is by researchers turning "to their own worlds of experience" (p. 10) as material to study. This view of interpretive inquiry not only allows for researcher subjectivity, it demands it in order for the reader to "connect" with the phenomenon under study. In discussing his own work on the experience of alcoholics, Denzin (1989) reveals;

> In my study of the alcoholic self, I went to places where alcoholics gathered, I presented myself as a person interested in A.A. I have alcoholic family members; I formed friendships with recovering alcoholics and their spouses and children. I also became friends with alcoholism counselors and other treatment personnel in treatment centers. (p. 55)

Building friendships with the key informants can provide the researcher a deeper understanding of the social process and the human experiences that are under study. This issue of researcher–friend dilemma also emerged in my research with Asian Indians.

Over the period of my predissertation study, I established special relations with some of my research participants. Our common identity as Asian Indians was undoubtedly the most important factor in this. Some of the children, as well as their parents, expressed interest in knowing about me and my family, and two of the children even wanted to see pictures of my family in India (which I did show to them). Ajay, a 5-year-old kindergartner who was very fond of drawing and painting, was very interested to know about my sister, who is an artist; thus, art or pictures became a way to open him up to share with me some of his views, not just about art but also about many other related things, such as his ambitions, his parents' expectations of him, and his relationship with his brother. I now ask this: What was the purpose and significance of these conversations about my family? Were these conversations a way to enable my participants to talk freely; or was I turning to my own world as material to study, in Denzin's (1989) view? Were these conversations actually a foundation for building friendships, or were they a combination of all of the above? I struggled and continue to struggle with the issue of the substitution of researcher–participant relationship for that of friendship. How ethical or unethical is it to continue having an association with my research participants after the formal completion of the study? And also, when does a study end formally? If I continue my relationship with my research participants, I grapple with the issue of considering my conversations with them simply as conversations between friends and not as additional data for my study.

RESEARCH OR PERSONAL QUEST?

"Qualitative research is an inquiry into the personal world of others that, if one is fortunate, becomes a journey into oneself. Qualitative inquiry offers opportunities for the researcher to inquire into oneself while inquiring into the other."
—Sears (1992, p. 147)

Why did I decide to study Asian Indian immigrants? What does my identity have to do with it? Is it expected of minority researchers to focus on minority issues? Why do minority researchers conduct most of the studies dealing with minority issues? Does belonging to a particular racial, linguistic, ethnic, or religious group make it easier or harder to study people in that same group? What are the issues involved in studying a particular ethnic minority, and how do those issues change when the researcher also belongs to the same group? All these and many other similar questions had been occurring and recurring in my mind after I decided the research area for my doctoral dissertation. While conducting the predissertation study, I got an opportunity to delve into the multiple sides of some of these questions. Besides being a pilot to explore a possible dissertation topic, the project was of special interest to me. Being an international student, I am myself struggling with issues of adjustment in a new cultural and educational setting. Doing this study gave me an opportunity to reflect on some of my own biases and beliefs about living in a foreign country. The time is not far off when my husband and I will make the final decision of whether to live in the United States and apply for immigrant status, or go to India after finishing our respective degrees. My research with Asian Indian families in the United States will undoubtedly force me to reflect on some of the issues pertaining to immigrant experience. I hope I will also be able to weigh my options in a somewhat different manner than most other international students in my situation, and also in a different light than I would have had I not conducted this research. In this way, both my predissertation research and my dissertation research are part of an important personal quest as well.

Once again, I am confronted with a dilemma of a different sort: the "so what" question in research. Should a research project answer only the profound and often abstruse questions that are (or at least are supposed to be) of significance to the community of practitioners, policymakers, researchers, and the community at large? Or can a research project be undertaken with an eye on resolving some of researcher's personal predicaments? Can a research project be a pursuit of a personal nature as well? If so, how practical, useful, and ethical it is? These are some of the questions that, in my opinion, demand critical discussion in the group of researchers who are equally as concerned with research methodology as they are with the results.

FINAL THOUGHTS

The process is always as important as the final product, and so is the case with research. Most researchers often get so involved with the mounds of raw data, stacks of copies of relevant literature, and files of data analysis that it is very easy to lose sight of the complexity and intricacies of the process by which they arrive at the final product. This is not to say that they do not plan their research methodology; in fact, the argument is just the contrary. Most research studies are done with very careful planning of the methodology, often to the last detail possible. The precisely written section on methodology in the published article or book is the manifestation of a carefully worked out and executed research design. In their zest to follow the planned methodology, many researchers tend to ignore the issues that emerge during the research process. These emerging methodological issues, I believe, are important sources of knowledge and must be reflected on and incorporated into the research design. The first step in this direction is to make the researchers aware of the presence of surfacing methodological details and to provide them with the opportunities to reflect on those details. This chapter has been a product of such a reflection process.

The question that now emerges is this: How accurate and important is such reflective writing? If we acknowledge that a researcher's subjectivity is a necessary and vital element of the inquiry process, should that not be a mediating factor in the text of the original research report? Arnold (1994) has addressed the issue of researcher subjectivity by suggesting the practice of incorporating a fieldworker's voice into research reports. I am now inclined to think that by incorporating some of my just-described thoughts and reflections in the text of my predissertation research paper (Mehra, 1996), I would have been able to provide my readers with an enhanced understanding of the experiences of Asian Indian children. In other words, my writing should have reflected the subgenre of

> impressionist tales [that] present the doing of fieldwork rather than the doer or the done ... [and that are] a representational means of cracking open the culture and the fieldworker's way of knowing it so that both can be jointly examined ... [by keeping] both subject and object in constant view. (Van Maanen, 1988, p. 102)

Having written this chapter, I now tend to agree with Krieger (1991):

> At one time I could write a study and then write separately about how, and why, I came to do it. I no longer feel I can proceed in that way. Writing about others, or about a social process, without reference to the self has come to feel alienating and untrue to me. Writing personally has become a way that I can feel I am doing social science in a responsible manner. (p. 2)

I wonder, however, if my dissertation committee would be willing to accept that kind of personalized writing in my doctoral dissertation.

REFERENCES

Arnold, J. C. (1994, November 10–13). *Telling an impressionist tale: Enhancing our knowledge of college students.* Paper presented at the 19th annual meeting of the Association for the Study of Higher Education, Tucson, AZ (ERIC Document Reproduction Service No. ED·375 #716)

Denzin, N. K. (1989). *Interpretive interactionism.* Newbury Park, CA: Sage.

Krieger, S. (1991). *Social science and the self: Personal essays on an art form.* New Brunswick, NJ: Rutgers University Press.

Kumar, N. (1992). *Friends, brothers, and informants: Fieldwork memoirs of Banaras.* Berkeley and Los Angeles: University of California Press.

Lather, P. (1992). Critical frames in educational research: Feminist and post-structural perspectives. *Theory into Practice, 31,* 87–99.

Lincoln, Y. S., & Guba, E. G. (1985). *Naturalistic inquiry.* Newbury Park, CA: Sage.

Mehra, B. (1996, April, 8–12)....": *Experiences of three Asian Indian children in a multicultural elementary school.* Paper presented at the 1996 annual meeting of the American Educational Research Association, New York.

Scheurich, J. J. (1994). Social relativism: A postmodernist epistemology for educational administration. In S. J. Maxcy (Ed.), *Postmodern school leadership: Meeting the crisis in educational administration.* (pp. 17–46). Westport, CT: Praeger.

Sears, J. T. (1992). Researching the other/searching for self: Qualitative research on [homo]sexuality in education. *Theory into Practice, 31,* 147–156.

Van Maanen, J. (1988). *Tales of the field: On writing ethnography.* Chicago: University of Chicago Press.

7

A Landscape with Multiple Views: Research in Pueblo Communities*

Anya Dozier Enos
Santa Fe Indian School

PARALLELS IN ACADEMIC AND PUEBLO THOUGHT

"A paradigm encompasses three elements: epistemology, ontology, and methodology" (Denzin & Lincoln, 1994, p. 99). Words like "paradigm," "epistemology," and "ontology" scare me and make me think I am less than comfortable in academia. And yet, I had professors (including Denzin) who explored the issues behind these complexities in such intriguing ways that what I learned through the university continues to fascinate me.[1] As I explored the issues of paradigms (without using these terms), I began to see that what academia calls "emerging paradigms" mirror traditional Pueblo beliefs about the world and how one knows the world.[2]

---

* Portions of this chapter appeared in my dissertation.

[1] Other writing that contains this jargon (Collins, 1991; hooks, 1990) has taught me much, but it is a struggle for me to read.

[2] I believe such academic language keeps people in Native communities from understanding that their traditional knowledge is similar to knowledge many university researchers now embrace. These researchers do not see the connection either, because they have made themselves inaccessible, in part, through their language. I wish to write in such a way as to be accessible to nonacademics. This means that the format of this chapter wanders some from a traditionally academic style. For example, after reading a few pages, definitions of *Pueblo*, *Indian*, and who I am will surface. Also, to honor the multivocal aspects of these explorations, I use a lot of footnotes.

Some of the research paradigms and perspectives that academia is currently discussing as "emerging" (in particular, see Denzin & Lincoln, 1994;
LeCompte & Preissle, 1993; Lincoln & Guba, 1985) are similar to ancient,
traditional Pueblo ways of understanding the world. As with these "new"
paradigms and perspectives, Pueblo people acknowledge that subjective
ways of knowing are valuable (and, in fact, that human beings are not—and
should not be—objective); that multiple, sometimes even contradictory,
viewpoints are possible and what is true may vary from person to person,
from culture to culture; that the stories people tell have multiple levels of
meaning, and each time these stories are told new knowledge is gained.[3]
Therefore it is both through my training as an academic researcher and as a
member of a Pueblo that I must recognize the importance of subjectivity and
multiple understandings in my research with Pueblo communities. In these
ways, I combine two of the multiple parts of who I am: Pueblo person and academic. However, the complexity inherent in this combination is not resolved; there are aspects of ambiguity in my roles both of Pueblo member
and academic, as well as in the intersection of these two. This chapter, based
on my experiences doing research in Pueblo communities, explores sorting
through the levels of comfort and discomfort I experience in these dual roles
(certainly realizing I have other roles as well: wife, mother, sister, daughter,
niece, aunt, employee, etc.).

My research interest is the education of Pueblo students, particularly the
influence of the community on students' approaches to mainstream education. Later in this chapter, as I explore my subjectivity in this area, I find I am
both a part of and separated from the Pueblo and from academia. The complexity of just these two elements of my identity hints at the complexity of
American Indian[4] identity in general. In feeling like I both belong and am
separate, I do not feel marginalized in that I never feel completely out of the
center of power in either arena; rather, there are times of comfort and times
of discomfort. Perhaps I am on the edge of center....

EXPLORING PUEBLO LANDSCAPE

I find it useful to begin with an explanation of *Pueblo* not only as a definition,
but also in order to recognize the multiplicity and complexity of how to gain
an understanding of the Pueblo using the mainstream, academic conven-
tion of a chapter in a book.

---

[3]Bakhtin (1981) also understood the importance of how meanings are reconstructed with each re-
telling.

[4]Most Pueblo people use the term *Indian*, not *Native American*; therefore, I use the term *Indian* in this
chapter.

Pueblo has come to have multiple meanings: it is a village, a community, a culture, a tribe, an Indian reservation. Life in the Pueblo radiates out from a center. Looking out from any Pueblo's plaza (in the center of the village), one sees distant mountains. Most of the year, these mountains have snow-covered peaks. Only in the middle of summer are the mountains free of white patches. In some Pueblos, the mountains loom large and not so far away; in others, they appear blue in the distance. In most Pueblos, between the plaza and the mountains are mesas (from the Spanish for "table"), raised land formations that are flat on the top. Near to most of the Pueblos is a river. The movement from plaza to river to mesa to mountains is a process that is necessary for hunting, fishing, farming, and gathering materials for pottery and ceremonial use (Jojola, 1996; Swentzell, 1992). These land formations, with their vegetation and animal life, are at the core of Pueblo being: "the landscape resonates the spiritual or mythic dimension of the Pueblo world even today" (Silko, 1986, p. 91). Pueblo people have been here since before Columbus, and everything Pueblos need to maintain their traditions are found here. The plants and animals traditionally nourish and clothe people; the earth itself is used to form pots to cook and store food. Stylized representations of the important animals and plants are found in rock art, on pottery, and in embroidery. The Pueblo, as a part of this geography, this flora, this fauna, is mirrored in traditional art forms; these art forms, in turn, root people in their Pueblos.[5] There is an interplay between nature, art, and tradition in which each serves to strengthen the other, and all work to attach people to their Pueblo communities. The core, the center of this world, the center of *the* world is the Pueblo plaza.

Traditionally, Pueblo Indian people live in small villages made up of apartment-like adobe structures. Agricultural fields are maintained within walking distance from this center. Most Pueblo Indian reservations include these traditional places of homes, fields, and mountains; however, housing, to meet the needs of expanding populations, is now extending beyond the traditional center. By and large, Pueblo people who live on the reservation live in housing areas with many nearby neighbors.

I live on the reservation, but my nearest neighbor is half a mile away. Although not unique, this situation is far from common. Living as I do, I am on the edge of the center of my Pueblo. There are reasons for why I live here. It is important for me to live on the reservation, and it is important to my husband, whose family were ranchers, to live where there is space between houses. My family history, as well, influences my place in the Pueblo, and my interest in Pueblo education.

---

[5]Spicer (1971) points out how these symbols are part of a subjugated people's persistent identity systems. Such symbols, then, bond people not only to their land, but also to each other.

SUBJECTIVE LINKS TO RESEARCH[6]

My paternal grandfather, Thomas Sublette Dozier, came to Santa Clara Pueblo from Missouri to teach at the U. S. government day school in 1893. Within 3 years, he had married a woman from the Pueblo and the first of their 11 children was born. Although it was against government policy, he encouraged the use of the native Tewa language in the classroom for the 5 or 6 years he taught. All of his children were raised as Pueblo people, speaking Tewa as their first language, Spanish as their second. They learned English only after several years at school. In a letter to a cousin (1919), my grandfather wrote:

> I think you know I married a Pueblo Indian woman. She had not even had any advantages of school. Yet with all her disadvantages—her lack of training and different ways from my own, I am still quite proud of her.

Although all of his children had experiences away from Santa Clara, all remained tied to the community, most living there at the time of their deaths.

My father, Edward P. Dozier, was the youngest child in the family. He was born in 1916. In the 20 years between him and the oldest child, important changes took place in the policies of educating Indian students. His mother, who was probably born in the early 1870s, had no formal education and spoke Tewa and some Spanish, but no English. Her younger sisters, however, went to a Catholic boarding school and a Bureau of Indian Affairs (BIA) day school. These sisters became trilingual and could write in English.

My father and the brother next to him in age were the only children in the family to complete high school. Their older brothers did not finish elementary school, and their two older sisters attended but did not complete high school. The oldest siblings spent a couple of years in boarding schools. When I was a child, they would entertain me with horror stories about their boarding school experiences: children crammed into one-room sleeping quarters; children getting sick and dying; staff beating children for small offenses such as speaking their native language. Although the two youngest boys attended a BIA day school when they were young, both graduated from a non-Indian Catholic high school. Uncle David went on to receive a BA; my father obtained a PhD. Both boys received their formal education first in Spanish (in public schools) and then English (in BIA and Catholic schools).

---

[6]The following section includes a short history of my father's family. My mother is a German immigrant who came to the United States when she was 5. Perhaps because I knew only my grandmother on my mother's side when I was growing up, perhaps because of the pull of the Pueblo, I have tended to focus on my father's side of the family. My German grandmother, however, was a fascinating person in her own right, but I will not embarrass my mother with details of her life here. My mother, while managing to strive toward her own life goals, has steadfastly supported the life pursuits first of my grandmother, then my father, and now me.

The language spoken at home was always Tewa. In fact, because my father was 9 when his father died, and 12 when he learned English, he was the only child in the family who never communicated with his father in English. However, learning English as a third language did not seem to adversely affect my father's and Uncle David's long-term school success.

As a family member, Pueblo member, and a teacher of Pueblo students, I have many questions about the school experiences of my relatives. Were my father's older siblings unable to go further in school because of negative experiences with formal education (they attended school at a time when assimilation was the goal)? Perhaps it was just differences in personality and/or historical times—the older siblings were economically self-sufficient and lived fulfilling lives. Why were the younger children in this family, who had less direct influence from their Anglo[7] father, more successful in U. S. schools? Were the younger children more successful because schooling policies had changed? Was the success due to their older siblings' support and empathy? Was it helpful that their mother had no experiences (negative or positive) with formal education? Was it significant that neither their mother nor they had gone to boarding school at a young age? These questions fueled my interest in the impact Pueblo families have on students' learning in mainstream American schools.

These family experiences have also created for me an ambiguity about formal education. What is the goal of formal education? Although assimilation[8] is no longer a stated goal, schooling still focuses on getting Pueblo people into the mainstream. As most of my father's family found, staying in the Pueblo provides a richer, fuller life than living in the mainstream. If schools only move Pueblo students away from their culture and toward the mainstream, they are destructive. However, schools can be valuable in helping the Pueblos maintain their sovereignty by educating Pueblo students to negotiate positive Pueblo/ mainstream relationships.

As I began my dissertation research, I was interested in how parents' attitudes toward education affected their students' performance in school. I assumed that the school experiences of grandparents and great-grandparents (particularly in boarding schools) would be negative. I wondered if this neg-

---

[7]During my grandfather's time in New Mexico, three categories were recognized: Spanish (referring to descendants of the Spanish colonizers of the 16th through 19th centuries), Indian, and Anglo. Since my grandfather was neither Spanish nor Indian, he was "Anglo." In the past 20 years or so, some "White" New Mexico residents, who are not of Spanish or Anglo descent, have questioned the limits of these three categories.

[8]Assimilation means to replace one culture (Pueblo culture in this case) with another culture (mainstream American culture in this case).

ative experience had colored the view of education for current students. My research purpose shifted, however. As I listened to what the study families were telling me, I saw themes that led in a slightly different but ultimately more interesting direction (LeCompte & Preissle; 1993; Lincoln & Guba, 1985). From the people I interviewed, I never heard a direct connection between grandparents' negative experiences with school and parents' and students' experiences. The older people echoed the horror stories I heard from my aunts and uncles, but they also balanced them with positive stories, such as developing lifelong friendships with people from different Pueblos. As people talked, a focus different from the negative legacy of boarding schools became apparent. When I reviewed the transcripts from my first interviews, I noticed a strong theme emerging, from all the participants. All the adults I talked with simultaneously encouraged their children to leave the Pueblo for a period of time, and also to return. The students I talked to confirmed this; they expected to leave and return. This leaving and returning intrigued me, and as I explored it with the people I interviewed, I found related topics: the importance of family, place, and identity in this pattern of leaving and returning. How all this affects students' approach to schooling became the heart of my research findings. Certainly, there is not space to elaborate on these findings; but later in this chapter, I touch just briefly on the influence of identity because it fits well with my musing about subjectivity and research.

There are some unique considerations to be taken into account when doing research in Pueblo communities. Any research proposal must go through proper channels. These channels vary from Pueblo to Pueblo, but the starting point is always the Pueblo governor. I went first to the governor of my own Pueblo for advice. He gave me a letter of support and introduction to take to governors of other Pueblos. In the communities in which I did my research, the governors all gave approval based on my proposal and the letter from my governor. In other cases, governors have asked their tribal councils to make the final decisions regarding research projects in their communities (Romero, 1994).

Another consideration is that there are parts of Pueblo life that are private and not to be taken out of that Pueblo. This means they should not be discussed with outsiders. The information must not be written or recorded in any fashion. Not knowing how parents and students view the impact of this private information on their formal education must remain a missing part of research. I respect both the orality and privacy of Pueblo tradition and believe that these customs are partially responsible for the strength and perpetuation of the Pueblo. Such information retains a certain vitality and appropriateness in the minds of our people because it is not recorded. Keeping information private eliminates the risk of misinterpretation by outside sources. It is only in the Pueblo context that such information has the meaning it is meant to have. Changing its form or removing it from its context within the Pueblo would distort and corrupt its meaning and, therefore, its critical value for Pueblo culture. The loss of such information may result in incomplete research, but it is a necessary incompleteness. What remains, however, is actually more compatible with what can be written for and understood by non-Indians who are interested in the education of Indian students in American schools.

I have tried to write in a style that is accessible to teachers and Pueblo members. As I mentioned earlier, I avoid using jargon whenever possible. I have struggled to read research from both the field of education and postmodern discourse. After picking my way through jargon-woven, paragraph-long sentences, I have found research that is both fascinating and tremendously useful in the classroom.[9] As a classroom teacher, I did not have time to read this kind of writing. It angers me that these ideas are not put into more accessible forms so teachers can quickly read current research. In this way, information is limited to certain groups, and kept from the group who could most benefit by it. Even though limiting information is a criticism of postmodern critique, their written explanations are inaccessible (Fine, 1994; Lather, 1991) to practitioners and so teachers are missing access to valuable ideas.

I have been careful to avoid incorporating jargon into my writing and speech for personal reasons as well. The way I normally talk[10] already cuts me off from certain levels of interaction in my home community. Informal social interactions (both in the Pueblo and in the mainstream) are difficult for me. I can blame my speech, or perhaps my speech is simply a result of being uneasy around people. At any rate, speaking in jargon would, I believe, further separate me from my community and family. I do not have confidence in my ability to switch back and forth between what is "regular speech" and "educationese."

Even without changing the way I talk, the work I did for my PhD, especially the research, has changed me in ways that I had not expected. When I first be-

---

[9]Phelan, Davidson, and Cao's (1991) research on the boundaries all students cross when they go from home to school and/or interact with peers is helpful to understanding why some of my students might excel in one environment (usually home or peer focused) but exhibit discomfort in other environments (usually school). Fordham's (1993) research, which postulates that African American students who excel in school may feel that they must also excel in an area acceptable to their peers (such as sports or humor), could be a possible explanation for some of my Indian students' behavior.

[10]Because I speak standard English, I am uncomfortable with some common Pueblo grammatical differences (such as "Eat good," a frequent utterance at feasts to encourage people to eat as much as they want); but I have other grammatical inconsistencies in my speech (such as ending sentences with prepositions) that are more common in mainstream "standard" English.

gan to develop interview questions and to interview people, I had trouble creating questions and finding places to probe for further information. In Pueblo culture, we—particularly women—learn to accept things, and not to question.[11] When I saw that my non-Indian colleagues (both at work and at the university) could more readily create questions and find places to probe, I was in awe. When I complained to my advisor about my inability to do this, he told me I would change; I have. What concerns me is that although I have gotten better at asking questions and encouraging people to elaborate, I cannot always turn off this questioning when I am in Pueblo settings where it is not appropriate. Certainly, I do not ask such questions aloud, but sometimes I can't stop the questioning that continues to go on in my mind. Feeling that I could absorb what was happening in traditional settings created an acceptance in me. These traditional occasions were comfortable, a time I could truly be calm. Now it is more difficult, and sometimes impossible, for me to get to that place, and I am less accepting of the world in general. This is a change I did not expect, did not want; even as I struggle against it, I am removed from Pueblo life in a subtle but important way.

Living in the Pueblo, one often feels that everyone knows everything about you, and that what you say to one person could easily be repeated to many others. Although I did multiple, in-depth, formal interviews with 10 students and their extended families from different Pueblos, I chose not to do participant observation because I did not want people to feel that everything they did and said might wind up in my dissertation. I distanced myself from people I was not interviewing because I did not want them to feel uncomfortable about my research. I was (and still am to some extent) uneasy about working toward a PhD, because that in itself, I thought, could somehow distance me from the Pueblo. I know now that it is not how other people interpret my actions, but rather how I see myself that has resulted in the change. Nonetheless, the change has occurred.

All of these issues—my being part of and separate from my community; my family; what I chose to include and exclude from my research and the data I gathered—all play into my subjectivity as a researcher. Peshkin (1988) encourages researchers to identify what aspects of their subjectivity are awakened in a given research setting. He identifies these aspects as "Subjective I's" (p. 18). One of my Subjective I's is the Outsider/Insider I.[12] As a woman who looks non-Indian, speaks differently, and yet has Pueblo family and community ties, I am simultaneously Outsider and Insider.

---

[11]Medicine (1988) discusses some of the unique challenges facing Native women in academia.

[12]Foster (1994) struggles with some similar issues as a researcher who is both an outsider and an insider; however, her "community" is African American teachers.

Where I have chosen to live exemplifies my Outsider/Insider status. I live on Pueblo reservation land, but my nearest neighbor is half a mile away. In a community where village life is important this is unusual (although not unheard of). Furthermore, my husband, who is Indian, but not from a Pueblo tribe, participates in traditional Pueblo doings that are open to him as an Indian man, but not to me as a Pueblo woman. Being a woman closes me off from some traditional information. Not speaking the Indian language further cuts me off from specialized Pueblo knowledge.

Knowing some of the language would help me to understand the culture at a deeper level. However, there are forms of the language that are very specialized and used only by men after decades of training. Therefore, I could know more about Pueblo traditions if I knew the language better, but there are some parts of Pueblo culture I could never know, both by virtue of being a woman, and because of language limitations. The same holds true for Pueblo students; those who speak their language will have more access to cultural knowledge, but only those who hold specialized positions will understand the culture in depth.

Although I do not long to know that which is the province of men, I do long to be a more complete part of my Pueblo community. There is pain in this, as I believe I would be more complete as a person if I participated in traditional life more fully. Yet, rather than spending years learning my tribal language, I have spent years earning an advanced university degree. In some ways, as I explained earlier, doing research has hindered my participation in my Pueblo; in other ways, it has expanded it. People I interviewed would pull me into their explanations— "You know how it is...."—and I would feel accepted and comfortable. This is seductive. I want to feel part of Pueblo life, and these people see me as belonging. Yet, just as no one truly knows another person, I could not truly know what it was that that person was expressing. Part of my job as a researcher is to hear how the people I interview experience formal education from their viewpoints, not how what they say supports my own personal views. As I wrote, I continually tried to focus on what my interviewees said, rather than what I saw and felt. To help maintain that integrity, I asked other Pueblo people (including some of the people I interviewed) to read my research findings to see if they "rang true" about Pueblo life as they knew it.

An implication of this Outsider/Insider subjectivity is that I need to be careful, on the one hand, not to overromanticize the parts of Pueblo life I believe to be beautiful; on the other hand, not to denigrate what I see as problematic because of the pain I sometimes feel when I am less a part of community life than I would like. Until I began this research, I was unaware of how much I am an outsider; paradoxically, and unintentionally, this realization has caused me to remain more distant from some traditions.

Writing has brought up some of my own identity issues. What part of me is Pueblo and therefore "belongs"? What part of me is my German mother and therefore makes me an outsider? What was I including when I explored the relationship of Pueblo identity to education because of my personal struggle with identity? What was I excluding? What was I seeing and hearing, or not seeing and hearing, because of my subjectivity? These are questions of which all researchers must be aware (Glesne & Peshkin, 1992; Roberts & McGinty, 1995), but the added piece of my very personal, very sensitive Outsider/Insider subjectivity made this a particularly challenging piece of the research. Was I seeing other people struggling with their sense of belonging because this is the struggle that I experience? Did issues of identity seem important because they validated my personal concerns; but, perhaps, were they not so important in the lives of those I interviewed? Originally, I focused on identity, but the themes I saw in the data really led more strictly to belonging than to identity. Once I had sorted that out, I was able to address identity issues, and see how they related to belonging. When I understood this relationship, I realized I had to return to some of the people I had interviewed to clarify my understanding of what they told me. I return to this discussion on belonging further on.

Another expression of subjectivity is my Self-Centered I (Peshkin, 1988). It is this aspect that ultimately is the focus of this chapter. In one way or another, the research I do is all about me, about my family, about the communities with which I identify. Denzin (1989) comments that all research is really about the researcher; however, in order for the research to be of value, it must extend beyond me and my situation. And, once again, I must be aware of when I start to intrude inappropriately on my research and its findings. As the "Instrument" by means of which the data are gathered and analyzed, I am in some way always present in this research. In the same way, it is imperative that the focus of the research—Pueblo schooling—be always present.

COMMITMENT TO SCHOOL/COMMITMENT TO PUEBLO

The problem that tribal leaders and educators identify in terms of Pueblo formal education is the dwindling number of students who commit fully to the traditions of the Pueblo, and the growing number of students who appear to commit to (or do well in) neither school nor Pueblo. At this point, it seems a useful technique for students to commit to the Pueblo over school, as Peshkin (1997) found to be the case. In my research I did not find these students; rather, the students I interviewed were all in varying stages of acculturation.[13] Acculturation was evident to some extent in students' Pueblos, and school had further acculturating influences on them. Dealing with these issues of acculturation, at the same time recognizing their attachment to their Pueblos, gave some students the appearance of not committing to school. I am not sure that that, indeed, is what is occurring. The students I interviewed all have some strategies for doing well in school, although not always academically, while remaining attached to their Pueblos.

There is a tension involved in this attachment. In Pueblo life, this tension appears in the form of feelings of intense belonging[14] coupled with feelings of inadequacy. The resulting feeling of "I belong, but I must keep learning," keeps people attached to and identifying with their communities. There are several ways this is done on a community level. Pueblo people, as a group, are past oriented (De Vos, 1995; Spicer, 1971). The people I interviewed verified this. Everything in the past (either prior to World War II, or before the coming of the Spanish) was better than it is now; people were able to be more traditional. In part, they say, it is because the Pueblos did not have mainstream culture intruding through the media prior to World War II. People can still strive for the ideal of the past, but because of modernization they cannot achieve it totally. The study families all made clear that they did not believe any Pueblo person could live his or her whole life without the influence of the mainstream, particularly in terms of electricity (and through it, mass media) or cars. This, they said, means no one could be completely traditional all the time. Therefore, in striving to maintain Pueblo traditions, people feel inadequate. School plays a role in keeping Pueblo people from their traditions, and because of this I believe it adds to their feelings of inadequacy.

On the other hand, there are rewards for participating in Pueblo traditions that create feelings of great comfort and belonging.[15] For example, when people dance for a ceremony, they often receive gifts from community members; elders speak to the dancers, thanking them for participating; and there is also the intrinsic reward of working hard with others in the Pueblo to produce the dance. Ideally, these feelings of belonging motivate people to continue striving for the ideal. This creates a focus, and these people resolve the tension associated with belonging in a greater commitment to one's

---

[13]Acculturation is the process of incorporating aspects of a foreign culture (in this case mainstream American culture) into one's native culture (the Pueblo, in this case). In the process of acculturation, unlike assimilation, the foreign culture does not replace the native culture.

[14]Pueblo people have a multitude of kinship and nonkinship ties that keep them connected to their communities in a variety of ways (Babcock, 1991; Ortiz, 1969).

[15]According to Maslow's hierarchy of needs (as cited in Coon, 1989), this is a basic need for human survival.

Pueblo. This belonging, then, anchors people strongly to their Pueblos. In anchoring people, does it also separate students from school?

One Pueblo mother I spoke with, Susie, had recently completed a humanities course at a community college. When I asked her to help me sort out this idea of the tension of feeling comfortable with one's role in the Pueblo versus the feelings of being inadequate, she compared it to the Greek idea of hubris. An individual's arrogant pride (hubris), the Greeks felt, could cause problems for people who came into contact with the arrogant person and ultimately would cause the destruction of the individual—like Oedipus, Susie said. In the Pueblos, if an individual has more personal power (or more possessions, or fame, etc.) than others, it can cause problems for the community. Therefore, it is the role of everyone in the community to assure this will not happen, and this is usually done by finding fault with the people who are sticking out, or by questioning whether they are really Pueblo people. Susie pointed out that there are cases of individuals who are well-known and well-respected in Pueblo communities for a particular strength or achievement, and yet are not subject to community members' criticism. These are individuals, Susie told me, who meet two conditions: The community sees itself as responsible for their strengths, and the community is benefitting from their strengths.[16]

De Vos (1995) says Indian students will not do better than their peers, either in their communities or in school, in order to maintain a homogeneous group. Sanctions, like gossip, keep people from excelling. Susie had a different view: What is sometimes viewed as jealous faultfinding is the natural process of the community protecting itself and individuals from the negative imbalance that results from a person being too visible as an individual. Not all individuals who excel receive censure, only those who potentially disrupt the community. Newmann and Oliver (1980) also support Susie's view that friction is not necessarily bad. They see friction as a way to air problems, bring the community close to address these problems, and achieve homogeneity through the solution to the problem. This may be true of the friction within the Pueblos, but it does not address the friction between the school and Pueblo.

I find Susie's explanation to be a useful way to view what is often reported as a negative "tearing down" of those Indians who succeed. De Vos (1995), for example, concludes that Native American group identity keeps students from succeeding in education and "tends to prevent economic or social mo-

---

[16]Romero (1994) explores the importance of Pueblo people using their strengths to benefit the community, and the relationship of this to formal schooling. Pueblo people, she says, recognize that all individuals have a strength, but it is only beneficial if it is used to help the community. She recommends schools use this approach by helping Pueblo students to identify and develop their "gifts" in such a way as to be useful to their communities.

bility" (p. 37). He believes the whole group needs to remain the same, and as no real options are seen for the entire tribe to succeed through education, no individual can succeed and remain part of the group.[17] However, in the Pueblos, sanctions may be used against any Pueblo person who is not conforming to Pueblo values, not just in terms of school experiences.

The jealous faultfinding that creates friction for an individual is often expressed as a questioning of a person's identity. Given a person's actions, does he or she really "belong" to that Pueblo? Such questioning, and the implied criticism that one is not behaving as one should, means individuals' lives are closely watched, creating the feeling one is living in a fishbowl or under a magnifying glass. Proper Pueblo behavior, such as traditional participation, is rewarded; improper behavior is punished. Both serve to let people know what is acceptable behavior, what limits exist. Although the "punishments," like gossip and questioning, can create discomfort and be a painful part of Pueblo life, they also serve to teach people proper behavior. The ultimate punishment is to be removed from the Pueblo. However, even as one's identity is questioned, even as one's commitment to the Pueblo is questioned, as long as one is allowed to participate in the Pueblo, one belongs. How students manage the discomfort of such questioning results in different styles of attachment to their Pueblos, which in turn affects students' commitment to education.

The families I interviewed all brought up the issue of Pueblo identity when they talked with me. In struggling with the tension of belonging within the Pueblo, these families are also struggling with how school affects that tension of belonging. With the help of other researchers (Chrisjohn, Towson,& Peters, 1988; Ogbu, 1987, 1989), the link between these two struggles may be usefully made. These researchers have differing viewpoints about identity and its influence on education. Each helps in exploring Pueblo experience with school, but none fully explains it. In addition to what the families say and what research has shown, it is also important to look at governmental policies (both tribal and federal) that impact Indian identity.

Chrisjohn, Towson, and Peters (1988) conclude, at least in the case of a Canadian tribe, that Indian students reject formal schooling because they need to strengthen their Indian identity before coming to terms with the

---

[17]Deutsch (1987) noted that Hispanics in northern New Mexico villages appeared to be following this pattern of not allowing individuals to succeed, but she felt something else was happening. She demonstrated the strength of the community to provide support for its members across a large geographical area (a "regional community") when family members had to leave the village to work for wages. Individuals who were successful economically also participated in this network; community was the focus, however, not individual difference. The Pueblos also support individual success when it benefits the community.

dominant culture. Many Indian students "stop out" of school, as opposed to "dropping out." Once these students affirm their Native identity, they can return to school as adults and do well. I believe the participants in my study are struggling to affirm their Pueblo identity, but that for Pueblo people this is a lifelong issue. Coupled with it is another lifelong issue of how to deal with the dominant society. Schooling, as an aspect of the dominant culture, is a piece of this.

Ogbu (1987, 1989) looks at the effect of mainstream American culture's dominance with respect to minorities' formal education. Involuntary minorities, such as American Indians, reject the dominant culture by defining themselves in opposition to it. They also recognize that they do not have access to the same opportunities as nonminorities. Therefore, Indian students reject formal education as an institution of American culture. An important aspect of their identity is rejecting that which is part of the dominant culture. Pueblo people do remove all European influence in their most traditional ceremonies, but I think the examples that follow demonstrate that on other occasions Pueblo people are trying to find ways to live their lives to honor their attachment to their Pueblos, at the same time incorporating aspects of American culture. Part of this, then, becomes the struggle of how to include or reject school in the lives of Pueblo students.

Indian identity and the friction between Pueblo and school is further complicated by government and tribal requirements. Because a trust relationship exists between individual tribes and the federal government, Indian people have some privileges that non-Indians do not (such as health care through Indian Health Services). At one point, the federal government tried to determine Indian identity, and thus who would be eligible for such services, by stating that anyone who could prove she or he was at least one quarter Indian was Indian. Many Indian tribes were disturbed by the federal government determining who was Indian, as this was in conflict with tribal sovereignty. Currently, the U. S. government recognizes tribal determination of identity; however, a person can be enrolled in only one tribe. All tribes have enrollment procedures, but the procedures vary from tribe to tribe. Because each Pueblo is considered a separate tribe, each Pueblo determines enrollment.

Enrollment procedures set out objective criteria for Pueblo membership. As I mentioned at the beginning of this chapter, there are problems with this "objectivity" in Pueblo communities. Traditionally, determining who was part of the Pueblo was done on a case-by-case basis. One of the women I interviewed felt that by creating rules that had to be followed without regard to individual circumstances, the Pueblos were no longer able to make decisions fairly.[18] Manent (1996) reminds his readers that democracy, with its focus on individual rights, has a way of doing this. The individual and his or her nuclear family feel placed in opposition to the community, rather than a part of the community. The community, then, does not take individual factors into account, but objectively applies the same rules to everyone. For the Pueblos, such a system undermines traditional values.

It is to the Pueblos' advantage to encourage feelings of community belonging, and the role of the U. S. government brings a conflicting element into this belonging. Even so, governments, be they tribal or federal, cannot legislate identity. However, self-identification is not a sound measure of Indian identity, either. A standard joke among Indian people is of a non-Indian telling with pride of a Cherokee princess in the family. It seems that at least once a year an Indian college student association will find that some non-Indian has received financial aid because he or she claimed Indian ancestry. For these reasons, most Indian people feel self-identification is an inappropriate way to determine Indian identity. As David Cornsilk (Cherokee) says, "I don't believe in the right of self-identification. I believe that's an assault on the right of the Group" (Reynolds, 1993, September 8, A1). Cornsilk advocates membership in a tribe as the determinant of Indian identity. This is not an appropriate measure for Pueblo identity, however. It is possible to be a full-blood Pueblo person who participates fully in traditional ceremonies and not be enrolled. Until recently, Hopi only enrolled people whose mothers were enrolled. Santa Clara Pueblo still enrolls only people whose fathers are enrolled. A child of a Hopi father and a Santa Clara mother could not have been an enrolled tribal member of either Pueblo, even though the child was fully Pueblo. It is also possible to enroll a child in some Pueblos even though that child lives in a city and has never been to the Pueblo, as long as parentage guidelines are met. Some Pueblos have blood quantum requirements (usually a quarter to a half degree of Indian blood from that tribe); others do not. In most Pueblos, residence and participation are not requirements for enrollment. Given that membership is a governmental identification, and sometimes, although not always, based on race, it is possible to be an enrolled tribal member and still

---

[18]The Indian Civil Rights Act of 1968 locks the Pueblos into following such rules. This can create problems. Some Pueblos will not allow members who are part of Pentecostal religions to live in their communities. This is in violation of the Civil Rights Act and these Pueblos could be sued by the Pentecostal members of their tribes. Although Pueblos can ask any tribal member to leave, people who are asked to leave could, theoretically, use the Indian Civil Rights Act to take their Pueblo to court. Because of tribal sovereignty, it is possible that the Pueblo could still prevail in such a case. This is a pragmatic reason why it is important that Pueblo people both want to belong and feel enough belonging that they do not "turn against" the Pueblo.

not be considered, in some situations, to be "from" that Pueblo; the converse is also true.[19]

Thus, it is possible to be not enrolled (or enrolled in a different tribe) and still be "from" a given Pueblo. When Indian children are adopted from outside the Pueblo, they may retain membership in their birth community. Therefore, if a Navajo baby is adopted by Pueblo parents, that baby may remain an enrolled Navajo; if a Laguna Pueblo baby is adopted in Santa Clara, that baby remains enrolled in Laguna. Those children, however, most likely will grow up speaking the language of and participating in the Pueblo of the adopted parents. Although everyone in the Pueblo knows these children are not connected biologically to that Pueblo, they are considered to be "from" the Pueblo. In some cases, Spanish-descent children have been adopted by Pueblo parents. These children can grow up to be considered as being "from" the Pueblo. However, if anyone in the Pueblo has hurt feelings, or adoptee becomes too visible in the community, these Spanish-descent people become easy targets and are accused of being "not from here." The same is true for non-Pueblo Indians who are married into a Pueblo. Because of the patrilineal aspect of most Pueblos, if a Pueblo man lives in his wife's Pueblo—if his wife is from a different Pueblo—the man and his children may not be considered to be from her Pueblo. If these Indian "outsiders" live and participate in the Pueblo, they may be considered "from" that Pueblo (earlier this century, such people could even be "naturalized" and enrolled in some Pueblos). Once again, they can be targets of the painful accusation of being "not from here." Every Pueblo has several families who are in at least one of these categories due to the extensive intermarriage between Pueblos and other tribes. For people who live in Pueblo communities, belonging is important. It is a source of respect, pride, and comfort; likewise, not to belong is to be alone. Because of the importance of the physical location of the Pueblo, belonging to the Pueblo is a connection to the past as well as a connection to eternity.

Dozier (1956) points out that the Pueblo goal is to maintain the natural balance and harmony of the universe.[20] Dancing, and other forms of tradi-

---

[19]In looking at the identity of the Mashpee—a group of people of Indian descent trying to become recognized by the federal government as a tribe—Clifford (1988) traces the complicating factors of government and cultural identification of *Indian*. In this case, *Indian* and *American* seem to be mutually exclusive categories. This is not the case for Indian people such as the Pueblos, who are already federally recognized. Indians are American citizens, as well as members of a tribe. The Iroquois, however, view themselves as citizens of their tribe first, and American citizens second (and some Iroquois do not acknowledge American citizenship). The Iroquois have their own passports, which are honored by many major countries.

[20]It is important to note, though, that it is out of a seeming asymmetrical relationship that this balance occurs (Ortiz, 1969). It is "unity through diversity" (Cajete, 1994, p. 35).

tional participation, and thinking good thoughts are part of expected Pueblo behavior. In fact, participation in ceremonies with good thoughts is essential for the balance to continue and the universe to remain in harmony. In doing this in concert with the entire Pueblo, the Pueblo is one; it is in the ideal, balanced state. The more one participates, the more levels of involvement a person has, the better are the consequences both for the Pueblo and the individual. But as inability to speak the Pueblo language fluently can limit involvement, so do demands on an individual's time and energy. School and work are examples of mainstream demands on Pueblo people's time and energy.

In the same realm where people are encouraged and welcomed to participate by the Pueblo as a whole, individuals may question, even challenge, others' identities. In a newspaper article, a Pueblo woman tells a reporter about attending the local BIA day school and being teased because "she was the only child who was not 'all Santa Clara.' "This woman's own daughter is now in kindergarten, and she has chosen to send her to a private school because "'I want to send her where she will be happy, comfortable and get a good education' " (Walker, 1995, October 9, p. A4). Although she is sending her daughter to school off the reservation, this woman continues to live in the Pueblo. It is possible that she feels removed and attached at the same time. School becomes a site that embodies the friction within the Pueblo for this woman. Some of the study families gave similar examples. In this way, the friction within the Pueblo is entering the arena of mainstream–Pueblo conflict with school at its center.

There seems to be a paradox involving Pueblo identity. The Pueblos believe they have maintained their traditions because they have not allowed access to outsiders. Defining outsiders, then, becomes important. With the continued influence of mainstream American culture, this defining of who is an outsider and, thus, who may damage Pueblo traditions, has intensified. The paradox is that Pueblo identification could become so exclusive that no one is Pueblo and therefore Pueblo traditions cease to exist. In the past, gaining a commitment to the Pueblo through assuring that people "belonged" (i.e., had similar ideas and approaches to the world) meant that the Pueblo remained homogeneous. People who did not conform to the Pueblo rules left (Dozier, 1970), thereby keeping the Pueblos small and manageable. Given the opportunity for more housing, given the U. S. government programs that are funded based on population figures, since the 1960s it has been to the Pueblos' financial advantage to allow Pueblos to grow. This, though, is in conflict with the Pueblos' traditional focus on balance.

The ways different people resolve the tension of belonging to the Pueblo, and mediating the outside world addresses this fear of losing traditions and keeps many people striving to be Pueblo. The tension between what is traditional and what is influenced from the outside becomes important in the landscape of Pueblo peoples' lives. In striving to keep Pueblo traditions, the mainstream American culture and its schools add another element of tension.

The paradox of identity, the ambiguity of school. I see it in my research; I see it in my life. The study families and I continue to struggle with these issues while committing in some way to both the Pueblo and formal education. Having earned a PhD, I continue to live in the Pueblo.

REFERENCES

Babcock, B. A. (Ed.). (1991). *Pueblo mothers and children: Essays by Elsie Clews Parsons, 1915–1924*. Santa Fe, NM: Ancient City Press.

Bakhtin, M. M. (1981). *The dialogic imagination*. Austin: University of Texas Press.

Cajete, G. (1994). *Look to the mountain: An ecology of indigenous education*. Durango, CO: Kivaki Press.

Chrisjohn, R.; Towson, S.; & Peters, M. (1988). Indian achievement in school: Adaptation to hostile environments. In J. W. Berry, S. H. Irvine, & E. B., Hunt (Eds.), *Indigenous cognition: Functioning in cultural context* (pp. 257–283). Dordrecht, Netherlands: Martinus Nijhoff.

Clifford, J. (1988). *The Predicament of culture: Twentieth century ethnography, literature, and art*. Cambridge, MA: Harvard University Press.

Collins, P. H. (1991). *Black feminist thought: Knowledge, consciousness, and the politics of empowerment*. New York: Routledge.

Coon, Dennis. (1989). *Introduction to psychology: Exploration and application* (5th ed.). St. Paul, MN: West Publishing Company.

Denzin, N. K. (1989). *Interpretive biography*. Newbury Park, CA: Sage.

Denzin, N. K. and Lincoln, Y. (Eds.). (1994). *Handbook of qualitative research*. Thousand Oaks, CA: Sage.

Deutsch, S. (1987). *No separate refuge: Culture, class, and gender on an Anglo Hispanic frontier in the American Southwest, 1880–1940*. New York: Oxford University Press.

De Vos, G. A. (1995). Concepts of ethnic identity. In L. Romanucci-Ross & G. De Vos (Eds.), *Ethnic identity: Creation, conflict and accommodation* (pp. 15–47). Walnut Creek, CA: Alta Mira Press.

Dozier, E. P. (1956). The value and moral concepts of Rio Grande Pueblo Indians. In Vergilius, Ferm (Ed.), *Encyclopedia of morals* (pp. 491–504). New York: New York Philosophical Library.

Dozier, E. P. (1970). *The Pueblo Indians of North America*. New York: Holt, Rinehart & Winston.

Enos, A. D. (1998). *Art of attachment: Community influence on Pueblo Indian students' experiences with school*. Unpublished doctoral dissertation, University of Illinois, Urbana-Champaign.

Fine, M. (1994). Working the hyphens: Reinventing self and other in qualitative research. In N. K. Denzin & Y. S. Lincoln (Eds.), *Handbook of qualitative research* (pp. 70–82). Thousand Oaks, CA: Sage.

Fordham, S. (1993). Racelessness as a factor in Black students' school success: Pragmatic strategy or pyrrhic victory? In H. S. Shapiro & David E. Purpel (Eds.), *Critical social issues in American education: Toward the 21st century* (pp. 149–178). New York: Longman.

Foster, M. (1994). The power to know one thing is never the power to know all things: Methodological notes on two studies of Black American teachers. In A. Gitlin (Ed.), *Power and method: Political activism and educational research* (pp. 129–146). New York: Routledge.

Glesne, C. & Peshkin, A. (1992). *Becoming qualitative researchers*. White Plains, NY: Longman.

hooks, b. (1990). *Yearning: Race, gender, and cultural politics*. Boston: South End Press.

Jojola, T. (1996, April). *Coming together.* Symposium conducted by Native American Studies Center, University of New Mexico, Albuquerque, NM.

Lather, P. (1991). *Getting smart: Feminist research and pedagogy with/in the post modern.* New York: Routledge.

LeCompte, M. & Preissle, J. (1993). *Ethnography and qualitative design in educational research* (2nd ed.). New York: Academic Press.

Lincoln, Y. S. & Guba, E. G. (1985). *Naturalistic inquiry.* Newbury Park, CA: Sage.

Manent, P. (1996). On modern individualism. Journal of Democracy, 7 (1), 3–10.

Medicine, B. (1988). Native American (Indian) women: A call for research. *Anthropology and Education Quarterly, 19* (2), 86–92.

Newmann, F. M. & Oliver, D. W. (1980). Education and community. In E. Steiner, R. Arnove, & B. E. McClellan (Eds.), *Education and American culture* (pp. 61–89). New York: Macmillan.

Ogbu, J. U. (1987). Variability in minority responses to schooling: Nonimmigrants vs. immigrants. In G. Spindler & L. Spindler (Eds.), *Interpretive ethnography of education: At home and abroad* (pp. 255–278). Hillsdale, NJ: Lawrence Erlbaum Associates.

Ogbu, J. U. (1989). The individual in collective adaptation: A framework of focusing on academic underperformance and dropping out among involuntary minorities. In L. Weis, E. Farrar, & H. Petrie (Eds.), *Dropouts from school: Issues, dilemmas, and solutions.* Albany: State University of New York Press.

Ortiz, A. (1969). *The Tewa world: Space, time, being, and becoming in a Pueblo society.* Chicago: University of Chicago Press.

Peshkin, A. (1988). In search of subjectivity—one's own. *Educational Researcher, 17* (7),17–22.

Peshkin. Al. (1997). *Places of memory: Whiteman's schools and Native American communities.* Mahwah, NJ: Lawrence Erlbaum Associates.

Phelan, P., Davidson, A. Locke, & Cao, H. T. (1991). Students' multiple worlds: Negotiating the boundaries of family, peer, and school cultures. *Anthropology and Education Quarterly, 22,* (3), 224–250.

Reynolds, J. (1993, September 8). Indian writers: Real or imagined. *Indian Country Today,* A 1, A3.

Roberts, S. & McGinty, S. (1995). Awareness of presence: Developing the researcher self. *Anthropology and Education Quarterly, 26* (1), 112–122.

Romero, M. E. (1994). Identifying giftedness among Keresan Pueblo Indians: The Keres study. *Journal of American Indian Education, 34* (1), 35–58.

Silko, L. M. (1986). Landscape, history, and the Pueblo imagination: From a high arid plateau in New Mexico. *Antaeus, 57,* 83–94.

Spicer, E. H. (1971). Persistent cultural systems: A comparative study of identity systems that can adapt to contrasting environments. *Science, 174,* 795–800.

Swentzell, R. (1992). *Children of the clay: A family of Pueblo potters.* Minneapolis, MN: Lemer Publications.

Walker, H. (1995, October 9). Modern Pueblo women: Identity. *Santa Fe New Mexican,* A 1, A4, A5, A6.

8

Asian Americans: Refuting the Myth, Changing Faces

Judy HeeSung Kim
University of Illinois at Urbana-Champaign

The label "model minority" has magnanimously been bestowed on Asian Americans by the dominant society. However, what few people choose to notice is that Asian Americans never asked for nor sought such an "honor." Moreover, in the eyes of most Asian Americans, they do not see themselves as "model" (Chun, 1995). The reality is that most Asian Americans left their beloved homelands for political and/or economic reasons, and if situations, experiences, and necessity had not impelled them to leave, they would have remained in their homelands (Takaki, 1989).

Therefore, it is imperative that the entire context of the Asian American experience be studied (Chun, 1995). In terms of social stratification, in order to analyze this myth of the model minority, it is critical to investigate education in relation to the attainment of status (Grusky, 1994; Hoy & Miskel, 1996). However, one cannot only study the traditional elements of status attainment. Merely analyzing occupational attainment, income, and education does not truly portray the attainment of status. An overlooked integral component is the structural model that states that economic and political systems influence opportunity for certain groups of people, limiting some at the same time enhancing others (Hurn, 1993).

Using the traditional method of the individual status attainment theory, this myth of the model minority in regard to Asian Americans has been received and accepted without question, doubt, or inquiry. Taking into account the economic undulations, political transformations, and racial volatility in the history of the United States, to make such sweeping conclusions and to accept them just as facilely is naive at best.

This chapter is presented in four parts. The first part surveys the literature; the second part includes the methodology considered best to conduct this study. The third section provides a detailed explication of the case study; and the fourth part summarizes the conclusions, as well as states some policy implications.

LITERATURE REVIEW

Utilizing historical and governmental data on Asian Americans and secondary studies conducted on the educational experiences of Asian American students, this section: (a) defines and discusses the elements and evolution of the myth of the model minority; (b) delineates a brief history of immigration trends and the presence of Asian Americans in the United States; and (c) displays current demographics of Asian Americans.

Model Minority Defined

Although the term *model minority* is sometimes referred to as the model minority theory, there is no theoretical construct to support this hypothesis (Macaranas, 1980; Wong, 1985). As is discussed more fully further on, the term was originally coined by journalists in the 1960s (Osajima, 1988). Exactly how a term that arose in popular culture became a theory in scholarly research is not a line of inquiry that is the focus of this chapter, but one that is to be discussed in a forthcoming paper. However, what is determined in this section by means of a survey of the literature are three phases that undergird the effects and reactions to the label model minority. Although there is no specific, formalized definition of this term, by studying the context in which model minority is discussed, three distinct areas of research in response to the myth of the model minority stand out. I divide and label these three areas of research as follows: (a) denial; (b) revision; and (c) reconstruction.

Denial.   As the title indicates, this first phase of research was in immediate reaction to the initial coinage of the term *model minority.* The label was widely accepted by the public without questioning the basis of such a claim (Macaranas, 1980; Osajima, 1988; Takaki, 1989). In my usage of denial research, although there is no clear sociological definition to be found, "model minority" is used in terms of status attainment. Asian Americans were lauded for acquiring middle-class values, white-collar occupational positions, and high educational achievement. In much of the research on Asian Americans during this initial phase, at least one of these elements was discussed (O'Hare & Felt, 1991; Okutsu, 1989; Suzuki, 1995; Watanabe, 1995). Therefore, although there is no theoretical construct to the myth of the model minority, theories of social stratification are used to replace the substantial lack of theory in the hypothesis. In response, researchers argue the lack of validation of this myth, utilizing the same tools of social stratification (Gold & Kibria, 1993; Hu, 1989; Kibria, 1996; Martinelli & Nagasawa, 1987; O'Hare & Felt, 1991; Okutsu, 1989; Sue & Okazaki, 1995; Suzuki, 1995).

Denial research is useful in refuting the myth of the model minority, but its utility is beginning to wear thin. A survey of the literature indicates that this refutation began in the early 1960s, when the term was first coined. However, in the beginning of the 21st century, the stereotype still exists in many minds, from friends to teachers to employers, and can and does still affect many Asian Americans negatively. More is required to combat this myth. While denial research theoretically attempts to refute the myth, acts of outright discrimination still occur.

Revision. Revision research is a direct response to these acts of outright discrimination. Despite the numerous proclamations of admiration for Asian culture and Asian Americans as a whole, when the cultures and peoples begin arriving in one's neighborhoods, schools, and social groups, actions contradict these words and the claims sound hollow. When the numbers were small, Asian Americans were dotingly, even affectionately, regarded. However, although Asian Americans barely constitute 3% of the entire population, the population has increased by over 100% within the last decade (*Asian and Pacific Islander concerns: Report of the study committee; Asian and Pacific Islander population in the United States: March 1991 and 1990;* Min, 1995). Moreover, many Asian Americans migrate to the larger cities; thus, they tend to reside in five major states: New York, Illinois, Texas, California, and Hawaii (Hing, 1993; Min, 1995). In other words, the perception may be that there are many more Asian Americans than there really are.

Despite this perception of a larger population, Asian Americans on the whole, have been a quiet group. In this silence, many incorrectly read that Asian Americans do not experience discrimination. Revision research is in response to direct acts of discrimination against Asian American students, particularly in higher education. Initiated in the mid-1980s, revision research responded to unfair admissions practices of many of the elite universities on the West and East Coasts. A sudden and considerable decline of admittance of Asian Americans into many of these universities led to an investigation by Asian American political groups, questioning the admissions policies as well as the admissions officers. This investigation found that due to this stereotype of the model minority, many admissions officers held numerous misconceptions of Asian American students, which may have influenced their decisions. But most astounding of all, the investigation also found that admissions policies were adjusted so that standards for admittance of Asian American students would be more strenuous. Several universities were officially found guilty of these discriminatory practices, although most others were found innocent (Chan & Wang, 1991).

Thus, much of the revision research concentrates on studying admissions practices and overall experiences of Asian American students at colleges and universities (Agbayani & Ching, 1993; Chan & Wang, 19991; Divoky, 1988; Escueta & O'Brien, 1995; Hsia & Hirano-Nakanishi, 1995; Li, 1988; Magner, 1993; Nakanishi, 1995a, 1995b). This type of research focuses preponderantly on proving that Asian American students are not the whiz kids that they are touted to be. Furthermore, in order to fight the discrimination that comes with the assumptions that there are no barriers to educational attainment, revision research attempts to prove that there are actual barriers, and that there are Asian American students who are failures.

Although this type of research is in direct response to the discriminatory practices in college admissions, this defense mechanism has proved fruitless in combating the stereotype of the model minority, for two overriding reasons. First, the propaganda convincing most people that Asian Americans were model was so successful that research proving otherwise was easily overlooked. The second reason for failure, when viewed holistically, is ridiculous in nature. By insisting that Asian Americans are not model (are not successful, can be failures), researchers were purposely "proving" and actually applying the cultural deficit model to Asian Americans. Obviously, a deeper line of inquiry is necessary to combat such pervasive, insidiously institutionalized racism.

Reconstruction.   Rather than refuting the myth of the model minority, following postmodernists, reconstruction research on Asian Americans shifts to deconstructing the dominant language. What this deconstruction entails is breaking down the language of the dominant group, which tries to keep society in a stratified structure so that it can remain on the highest rung of the socially constructed hierarchical ladder (Jaggar, 1988; Tong, 1989). By protesting against and attempting to refute the myth of the model minority, the starting point assumes that the oppressors are setting the definitions and standards and that these definitions and standards are those by which to be measured.

Therefore, in reconstruction research, the term *model minority* is deconstructed and given little credence in the academic literature. *Model minority* is acknowledged as a term that has been applied to Asian Americans by the dominant group. Thus, the term is given its place in its historical and political context, but the researchers refuse to dignify the term by arguing or refuting the stereotype. Rather, the emphasis is on redefining Asian Americans as individual peoples by these individual peoples (*Asian and Pacific Islander Concerns*, 1987; Chun, 1995; Chun & Zalokar, 1992; Espiritu, 1992; Fong, 1995; Gold & Kibria, 1993; Hartman & Askounis, 1989; Kibria, 1996; Kim, 1973; Lee, 1994; Liu & Yu, 1995; Pang, 1990; Suzuki, 1995; Takaki, 1989; Ueda, 1990). The importance lies in claiming individual cultures, experiences, beliefs, and values within the Asian American label, and contextualizing each experience within each specific historical time period, social setting, political atmosphere, and economic condition.

Being lumped together under one political label by the dominant group, despite the differences within each ethnicity, removes any sense of power and self from the individual groups. The action of taking back, self-defining, self-identifying, and reconstructing the stories returns the power and focus to the people themselves. This became the focus of research during reconstruction research. Instead of researching Asian Americans under their politically defined label, the focus is on separate ethnicities, allowing the individual peoples to speak for themselves, about themselves. Distinctions, similarities, differences, barriers, and successes are accounted for and accepted.

Within this context, keeping in mind these three modes of defining the model minority, research on Asian Americans may be better understood. This chapter favors the philosophy, style, and methods of reconstruction research, but keeps in mind the utility and contributions of denial and revision research. Without the evolution and discussions of denial and revision research, reconstruction research would not hold as much merit or strength.

Domination in the United States

The United States has a long history of domination of its peoples, from its very inception in the near genocide of Native Americans to the forced amalgamation of all who are not White. In this manner, the United States has been a country that imposes its will in a fashion similar to the way the children's game "King of the Mountain" is played.

> The emphasis placed in the West on the notion of will as the essence of the person leads to a peculiarly Western notion of the individual ... Essentially, the Western notion of the individual is that of a separate, distinct entity in natural conflict with other such entities. (Hodge, Struckmann, & Trost, 1975, p. 26)

Keeping this concept of will in mind, for the oppressed peoples of color in the United States, as recipients of forceful will, domination takes on a special form, culminating in internalized oppression. Yamato (1990) recounts internalized oppression occurring when

> [m]embers of the target group are emotionally, physically, and spiritually battered to the point that they begin to actually believe that their oppression is deserved, is their lot in life, is natural and right, and that it doesn't even exist. (p. 20)

Predominantly, this country has used racism to enforce domination and oppression. One form of racism, and one that is most specifically internalized, is stereotyping. Negative stereotypes have been found to have harmful effects on self-image, as well as being a self-fulfilling prophecy (Sue & Kitano, 1973). "[M]embers of oppressed groups often believe that the source of their problems lies not in the structural relations in society but in themselves, in their own inadequacies and inabilities to be anything other than what the dominant image describes" (Osajima, 1993, p. 83).

For Asian Americans, racism has developed in a special form that, at the outset, may not appear to be negative. This special endowment is the myth of the model minority.

> By comparing how minorities as disadvantaged groups are doing relative to each other, the tendency is to view Asian Americans as a 'model minority.' This practice programs us to ignore structural barriers and inequities and to insist that any problems are simply due to different cultural values or failure of individual effort. (Woo, 1989, p. 185)

A survey of previous immigration laws belies much of the present-day historical amnesia. All the opulent praise poured on Asian Americans about their work ethic and the value placed on education cannot hide the procession of laws that had historically been enacted specifically to prevent the immigration of Asians into this country. The following is a brief list of various laws of exclusion.

- 1882 - Chinese Exclusion Act: Denied naturalization and immigration rights to the Chinese.
- 1907 - Gentleman's Agreement: The Japanese government agreed to stifle emigration of their people as long as the United States agreed to allow the entry of immediate family members of those already in the country, as well as promised to control blatant anti-Japanese acts and legislations.
- 1917- Immigration Act: Banned emigration from all countries in the Asia-Pacific Triangle except for the Philippines, (a U.S. territory) and Japan.
- 1922 - Cable Act: Stripped citizenship from any woman who married an Asian immigrant.

- 1924 - Immigration Act: "restricted annual immigration from all countries to 2 percent of the countries' national origin populations living in the United States in 1890, with an overall cap of 150,000, and also specifically banned immigration of persons who were ineligible for citizenship, i.e., Asian. Since immigration from all other Asian countries had already been halted, this provision appeared to be targeted at the Japanese" (*Civil Rights Issues Facing Asian Americans in the 1990s*, 1992, p. 4).
- 1934 - Tydings-McDuffie Act: Despite its being a territory of the United States, the people of the Philippines were only given commonwealth status and citizenship allowed only to those born in the United States. This act limited emigration to only 50 immigrants from the Philippines per year and did not allow entry of immediate family members of those already in the United States.
- 1935 - Repatriation Act: Gave a one-way ticket back to the Philippines as long as immigrants did not return.
- 1952 - McCarran-Walter Act: Lifted the ban on Asian immigration and granted naturalization rights for the first time, but still retained the national origins system.
- 1965 - McCarran-Walter Act: Finally removed the national origins system. The U.S. government allowed a quota of 20,000 immigrants per country, with a preference for highly skilled workers. (Chun and Zalokar, 1992; Lesser, 1985; Okihiro, 1994; Strouse, 1988; Takaki, 1989;)

As can be seen, racism against Asians has been reinforced outright by the legal system based on "democracy." Laws have been cleverly enacted in deliberate attempts not only to stop the flow of immigration of Asians into the United States, but to remove those already residing in this country as well. These laws are in clear contrast to the proclaimed benevolent attitude toward Asian Americans.

Cultural Conflicts

During the rise of the civil rights movement, the myth of the model minority developed full-blown. In the 1960s, the media produced reports on the success stories of Asian Americans who had immigrated to the United States, the same as other immigrants, but marveled at how they, above everyone else, were able to succeed (Osajima, 1988). The motive for this sudden respect for Asian Americans is quite suspect when one realizes that it was at this time that the civil rights movement was gathering strength in proving the racist foundations of White America. Hence, by uplifting the Asian Americans, with the help of the media, dominant society was trying to discredit the movement's strength (Osajima, 1988). They used Asian Americans to reaffirm the myth that the United States "is the land of opportunity, where people are rewarded for their hard work and diligence" (Osajima, 1988, p. 169).

Clearly, political and economic motivations affect the types of stereotypes that are popularly represented. When jobs are threatened, when wars erupt, Asians are viewed as a "yellow peril" or an "Asian invasion," but in times of political and economic equanimity, they are "model minorities." These seemingly random labels are structural elements "that assign to Asian Americans, and indeed to all minorities, places within the social formation. Further, the designations, the roles, and the relationships function to institute and perpetuate a repression that begets and maintains privilege" (Okihiro, 1994, p. 34).

It is highly suspicious that when just a decade earlier laws had been desperately enacted to remove and keep out Asian Americans, a sharp turn toward benevolence would develop. The model minority myth clearly has a motive behind its evolution. The main purpose was to inhibit the growing strength and increasing accusations of African Americans who were demanding their fair share, which had previously been denied them. However,

> [w]hat emerges is an evolving process of reification: first, a portrait of success is rendered; that image of success is reified into a reality deemed beyond dispute; then a search begins for the success-inducing elements in the reified reality. (Chun, 1995, p. 98)

Furthermore, Okihiro (1994) gives a clear picture of the structural construct for Asian Americans within White American culture:

> It seems to me that the yellow peril and the model minority are not poles denoting opposite representations along a single line, but in fact form a circular relationship that moves in either direction. We might see them as engendered images: the yellow peril denoting a masculine threat of military and sexual conquest, and the model minority symbolizing a feminized position of passivity and malleability. Moving in one direction along the circle, the model minority mitigates the alleged danger of the yellow peril, whereas reversing direction, the model minority, if taken too far, can become the yellow peril. In either swing along the arc, white supremacy is maintained and justified through feminization in one direction and repression in the other. (pp. 141:142)

It is apparent that although the attitude that is currently presented to the general public concerning Asian Americans is one of welcome and admiration, a quick review of reconstructed history would show that this attitude is an ephemeral stance at best.

Demographics

Population Changes.   As a result of the 1965 McCarran-Walter Act, whereas previously there had been few Asians in the United States, the population rose drastically from 1970 to 1980 and from 1980 to 1990 (Table 8.1).

As Table 8.1 indicates, the Asian American population increased 164.6% from 1970 to 1980 and 107.8% from 1980 to 1990. However, despite the exorbitant rate of increase, as of 1990, Asian Americans still represent only 2.9% of the entire population; thus, the sense of Asian invasion is highly unwarranted.

TABLE 8.1

Changes in Asian and Pacific Islander American Population,
1970–1990

	1970*	1980%	Increase from 1970 to 1980	1990	% Increase from 1980 to 1990
Total U.S. population	203,211,926	226,545,805	11.4	248,709,873	9.8
Asian Pacific Islander population	1,439,562	3,550,439	164.6	7,273,662	107.8
Asian Pacific Americans as % of total population	0.7	1.5		2.9	
Chinese	436,062	806,040	84.8	1,645,472	104.1
Japanese	591,290	700,974	18.5	847,562	20.9
Filipino	343,060	774,652	125.8	1,460,770	88.6
Korean	691,550	354,593	412.9	798,849	125.3
Indian		361,531		815,447	125.6
Vietnamese		261,729		614,547	134.8

Note. From *Asian Americans: Contemporary Trends and Issues*, by Pyong Gap Min, ed., 1995, London: Sage, Table 2.3, p. 16.

Employment and Socio-Economic Status (SES).   Many Asians naively emigrate with the "American Dream" in mind, with the hopes of striking it rich. In addition, 1965 immigration law emphasized technical/professional skills, and many Asian immigrants were professionals in their homeland. Despite these skills, on entry into the United States, with limited English abilities and faced with racism, they learn that opportunities are blocked (Takaki, 1989).

Although a cursory glance would show that economic conditions do not appear to reflect blocked opportunities, a closer analysis must be conducted for a full understanding. The median earnings of employed full-time Asian American males, with 4 years of high school completed, was $21,060, compared to $26,530 for White males. After 4 years of college, Asian American males earned $37,550 but White males earned $41,660 (*Asian and Pacific Islander Population in the United States: March 1991 and 1990*, 1992). Hence, despite the high number of Asian American males in white-collar sectors, they earn considerably less than the White male.

In addition, in terms of overall economic equity, although the national per capita income is $14,143, the per capita income of Asian Americans is $13,806. One must also keep in mind that most Asian American families have dual incomes. In fact, 20% of Asian Americans have three or more workers in each family (*We the American ... Asians*, 1993). Moreover, Asian American families experience a high percentage at the poverty level, an average of 22.3% (Table 8.2). Furthermore, when broken down by ethnicity, the variations are extreme, as low as 3.4% for Japanese Americans and as high as 23.8% for Vietnamese Americans.

Therefore, it is imperative that when analyzing economic trends for Asian Americans, issues such as ethnicity, gender, number of wage earners per household, and income in relation to years of education are all taken into consideration.

Family. Baumrind's (1989; 1991) classifications of authoritarian, democratic, and permissive style of parenting, Asian parents are found to fall in the categories of authoritarian and permissive style (Pai, Pemberton, & Worley, 1987). Briefly, the authoritarian parent is very strict, inflexible, and quick to punish. The democratic parent keeps the child's concerns in mind and even allows the child a voice in family matters. The permissive parent does not set any limitations or monitor behavior. Thus, a combination of the authoritarian and permissive style may leave the adolescent confused and angry (Baumrind, 1989; 1991).

There are many differences between Asian and American culture. Overall, the Asian child is traditionally expected to be blindly obedient and always, unquestioningly to defer to the wishes of the parents. Unfortunately, the entrance into a completely different culture changes many things, especially traditional roles. Yet without the exposure to White American culture that children receive in schools, parents do not know or are unwilling to accept these differences (Hurh, 1990; Kitano & Rogers, 1988; Sue & Kitano, 1973). For instance, with the child better able to learn English at school, there may be times when parents may need to ask the child to explain or translate; thus, there may be a role reversal in which parents may feel their position or authority is undermined (Chun & Zalokar, 1992; Hurh, 1990). Moreover, the child is then placed in a situation and role that he/she may not necessarily want, or even for which he/she is unprepared (Baumrind, 1989).

TABLE 8.2

Indicators for Economic Status for Asian Ethnic Groups in Comparison to Other Groups

Group	Median Family Income	% of Families at the Poverty Level
White	$37, 152	7.0
Black	$22, 429	26.3
Hispanic	$25,064	22.3
Asian and Pacific Islander American	$41, 251	11.6
Chinese	$41, 316	11.1
Japanese	$51,550	3.4
Filipino	$46,698	5.2
Korean	$33,909	14.7
Indian	$49,309	7.2
Vietnamese	$30, 550	23.8

Note. From Asian Americans: Contemporary Trends and Issues, Pyong Gap Min, ed., 1995, London: Sage, Table 2.9, p. 28.

Another conflict occurs because Asian parents do not express physical affection or give verbal rewards and encouragements as do White American parents (Freeman, 1993; Hurh, 1990; Pai, Pemberton, & Worley, 1987), but the Asian American child is socialized to believe that outward demonstrative behavior is the norm. Furthermore, because Asian parents expect docility from the child, their idea of communication is "a one-way communication by parents in which rules are explained to children rather than an open two-way exchange of questions and answers between children and their parents" (Pai, Pemberton, & Worley, 1987, pp. 15:16). In contrast, "the youth expect consistent rules and regulations. On the contrary they see their parents as holding two sets of rules; one for the children and one for adults" (Pai, Pemberton, & Worley, 1987, p. 8). Therefore, the traditional Asian side of the youth conflicts with the dominant culture of open communication that they learn in the schools, thus leading to a sense of isolation (Kitano & Rogers, 1988; Sue & Kitano, 1973; Pai, Pemberton, & Worley, 1987).

Generally, two contrasting cultural views, person-centered perspective and relationship-centered perspective, exacerbate the conflict. The adolescent holds the person-centered perspective of the American culture, in which the individual is the most important. The Asian parent holds the opposite view, that of the relationship-centered perspective in which others are viewed in hierarchical terms with specific rules, rights, and duties (Pai, Pemberton, & Worley, 1987). It is clear that the two differing views would produce discord in values, relationships, attitudes, identity, socialization, and cognitive style.

> The adolescents are caught in a tug-of-war between two cultures of many opposite norms ... [I]t is clear that the youth do not want to forego their Asian heritage. Rather, they appear to want to integrate it into their perceptions of their current lives. However, more traditional Asian ways tend to impose restrictions on the youth, which their Caucasian peers do not have to face. (Pai, Pemberton, & Worley, 1987, p. 14)

Because Asians emphasize familial interdependence, a student's success is not seen as an independent achievement, but rather as a reflection of the family's status (Freeman, 1993; Kitano & Rogers, 1988; Sue & Kitano, 1973).

School.   Studies show that Asian American students tend to have high grade point averages, with low test scores (Pai, Pemberton, & Worley, 1987). Thus, one may assume that despite the fact that the test scores show poor learning, because teachers view Asian American students through stereotypes of the model minority, they give them higher grades. Although at the outset this leniency may provide immediate gratification from good grades, for the students, in the long run, they are being hurt, as no true learning is accomplished. Moreover, in seeing them only through racial characteristics, by depersonalizing the Asian American students, the teacher does not see the individual (Chun & Zalokar, 1992; Sue & Kitano, 1973; Sue & Okazaki, 1995).

In addition, there is a tendency for Asian students to learn by direct rote memorization, which differs greatly from the White American system of individual methods of critical thinking. Pai, Pemberton, & Worley (1987) have concluded that the students' "teaching–learning style may be more didactic (directive) than dialogical (indirective), [thus] new programs and activities may be needed to be introduced in a more closely structured approach" (p. 31). Clearly, despite the stereotype of the bright Asian student, the mode of learning is different from that taught in the American schools and the actual success rate of Asian American students is not as solidly guaranteed as the myth holds.

Identity and Ethnicity.   For the Asian American student, ethnicity is indelibly tied to identity. Asian American students face a dilemma in that they are raised in White American culture but are pulled by Asian traditions. This dichotomy is sometimes difficult to understand, even for the students themselves. However, studies conducted with high school and college students show that at a very literal level they understand that they are Asian, and, in being Asian, they are different; but they resent the negative stigma associated with difference (Hurh, 1990; Osajima, 1993; Sue & Kitano, 1973; Sue & Okazaki, 1995; Suzuki, 1995).

This conflict is compounded by the various stereotypes imposed on the Asian Americans. Although the message is that all that is White American is good, the images of Asians can vary from the yellow peril to the model minority. Because of these stereotypes, Asian American adolescents are denied the opportunity to find the real self. Most often, what occurs is a sense of invisibility (Tajima, 1989). "The search for an identity is ... usually a search for that lost, pure, true, real, genuine, authentic self, often situated within a process of elimination of all that is considered other, superfluous, fake, corrupted or Westernized" (Minh-ha, 1990, p. 371).

METHODOLOGY

Many of these misconceptions regarding Asian Americans have evolved from incorrect analyses of statistical data. There are two popular datasets in the field of education that are used to describe the experiences of students in the United Stat   es: the 1980 and 1984 High School and Beyond (HS&B) Study, and the 1988, 1990, and 1992 National Educational Longitudinal Study (NELS). Just as the statistics claim the middle-class status of Asian American families but ignore the average of three incomes required to attain that status, HS&B and NELS have several shortcomings with regard to Asian American students as well.

In its categorization of the Asian American subpopulation, HS&B has a bias. The entire population of Asian American students in this study consists only of Chinese, Japanese, and Filipino students. This category overlooks Korean, Vietnamese, Asian Indian, and Hmong students, just to name a few. Chinese, Japanese, and Filipino Americans constitute the oldest group of Asian Americans in the history of the United States. By concentrating only on these groups, the new immigrant and refugee groups, which constitute an increasing number of Asian Americans, are overlooked. By ignoring such a huge group, a large portion of the Asian American experience is left untold. Statistically, this bias then leads to skewed and even false results, especially when considering that the findings will be applied to Asian American students as a whole.

In addition, the more recent longitudinal study, NELS, has gained popularity. At first sight, NELS corrected the bias of HS&B by incorporating more ethnicities as well as weighting the Asian American students to avoid the possibility of bias due to the small numbers. Thus, compared to HS&B, NELS proves to be more valid when utilizing statistics to determine the experiences of Asian American students. However, when analyzing the questions asked in the data set, the study is found to be imbued with White middle-class values. Some of these questions ask if the family has items such as a computer or encyclopedia, or whether the students have a separate room in which to study. Only those families in the middle class have such luxuries. Furthermore, the acquisition of the aforementioned objects implies that these items are necessary to be a good student, although most families in other countries do not have such luxuries yet produce many intelligent students.

Due to these popular statistical research claims that insist on highlighting the success of Asian American students, a qualitative approach is necessary to determine its validity as well as to cover areas that the statistics have overlooked (Denzin, 1989; Fraenkel & Wallen, 1996; Schatzman & Strauss, 1973). It is at this point that I wish to begin my study. Because the literature review described the true history of the Asian American experience in the United States, I chose to limit myself to one ethnicity in order to avoid overgeneralizations that come from studies on Asian Americans as a whole. I conducted a case study of the educational experiences of a group of Korean American students at a large university, in order to describe the difficulties that these students may face, which the statistical analyses do not explain.

In this case study, I conducted fieldwork by observing weekly, nonrequired Korean drum classes for a semester. As a Korean American, I was able to blend in easily and observe with only the slightest waves of curiosity from the rest of the group. The value of this study is in its richness of detail from observations and participation.

The class I chose to observe was one that is supported by the university, but not an official instructional class. The limited numbers of Korean drums were provided by the university, and the class was held weekly for 2 hours, in the basement of the university's Music Building. At its smallest, the group consisted of 11 students, and at its maximum, 18, with several students sitting out because of a shortage of instruments. The female to male ratio was about 2 to 1. Less than half were undergraduates, which the older students explained is a new phenomenon; previously, the younger students had never shown a particular interest in learning the instruments. There was one Asian Indian female, one White female, and one second-generation Korean American female. The rest were either international students or first-generation immigrants. Except for the aforementioned three females, everyone's native tongue was Korean. Moreover, during the social gatherings that took place after the class, although not everyone participated, there were always a few students who joined the gathering who had not been in the class; thus, the number in the social gathering did not differ much from the class size.

Seen on entry to the classroom, the room, itself, was quite unexceptional. The chairs and the music stands were shoved unceremoniously to the three walls, leaving the wall with the chalkboard open. The drums were piled neatly on the middle of the floor, and as the students entered, they chose an instrument and found a space on the floor to situate themselves. As with the chairs and the stands, the students would make a rough semicircle, with the opening facing the chalkboard.

The various drums were wrapped in individual cases, and the early arrivals, while waiting for the others, would take them out of the cases and tighten up the strings that held the skin, practice, and warm-up. Thus, within minutes, as most of the students entered, the small room would be filled with the deep resonating sounds of the drums. While the students were practicing, Hyung, the instructor, would draw on the chalkboard the notes of the musical pieces they would be working on that day. Almost exactly at seven, he would begin instruction.

FIELD RESEARCH

Initially, the idea of observing a Korean drum class in order to understand Korean international students' experience was rather daunting. Fortunately, I came to the realization that university life was not limited to the educational experience only, and that the social aspect played an important part as well. In fact, for some of the students, the Friday nights with the drum class and the social gatherings afterward comprised their total social activity for the week. Many of the students in the group did not join us in the gathering after the class, and when I asked why they did not, they explained that they had to return to study. Because they were international students, with English as their second language, the readings were not as easy as for native English speakers. Therefore, besides going to class and studying, they explained to me, they did not have much time to do anything else. Sometimes, if they had had a difficult week, they could not even take the time off for the 2 hours of drum class. All of this they told me matter-of-factly; after all, first and foremost, they were students.

This behavior, I found, could not be applied to Korean Americans. In the drum class there was only one Korean American student, but with my knowledge of various other Korean American undergraduate students, I can safely say that they do not have the same level of intense determination as the international students. This difference in attitude could be accounted for by their youth or possibly by their American influence, or one could look at it from the perspective of the international Korean students. The intensity of the international Korean students could be attributed to the fact that they were taking a big risk in studying abroad, thus they have more to lose. In any case, in order to make any conclusive determination, a more intensive comparative analysis of Korean international students with more Korean American students as respondents, would be necessary.

This knowledge about the Korean international students gave me newfound respect for their determination and quiet, uncomplaining persistence. Through mere observations of the drum class, one would not have been able to glean such information. Only through casual conversations during breaks and after the instructional phase was I able to learn about these experiences. Therefore, I realized how limited my thinking had been in assuming that in observing a Korean drum class, I would literally be observing only a drum class.

The drum class, itself, yielded more than one would have thought. After more observations, I was able to note that many repetitions occurred in people's behavior and even speech. Although the lessons were taught in almost the same format every week, some people's personalities began to show more strongly than others. These differences I was able to determine by the way they played the drums. On learning a new piece, some would timidly hit the new notes, afraid of making a mistake; others would boldly strike the drum skin, heedless of any errors they made; some would become flustered in having to play a solo in front of the class, but others would comfortably beat off the notes as if the student and teacher were alone in the room; some listened attentively to the teacher, others would allow their attention to wander. Furthermore, through brief talks with the teacher and a couple of students, I learned that the teaching of the drum class, itself, had a great deal of importance in its political context in Korea. They explained that during the period of Japanese colonization and even afterward, with the numerous military takeovers in Korea, higher education held more than an attainment of a diploma. It was at the university level that many protests were established and many concerns brought to light. During the strictest regimes, the learning and the playing of the drums, a spiritual symbol of freedom and unity among the people, was forbidden; yet many continued to do so.

From the onset of the 20th century, beginning in 1910 with the colonization by the Japanese, the people of Korea have known no independence from subjugation or freedom from oppression. From 1910 until 1945, the Japanese held Korea as a colony. The people of Korea were practically slaves to the Japanese. They were forced to speak, read, and write in Japanese, work in menial labor jobs for Japanese industries, and produce goods to supplement the needs of Japan (Kim & Roemer, 1980). Then, at the end of World War II, with the decision of the United Nations, Korea became a divided country; the North belonging to the Soviet Union and the South to the United States. Even then, South Korea experienced great political strife. From Syngman Rhee to Chang Myon to Chung Hee Park to Chun Doo-Hwan Roh Tae Woo—all titled "presidents" under the "democracy" determined by the U.S. government—the Korean people were governed by a strict dictatorship, with constant military coup d'états shaking the already tenuous government (Choy, 1979; Mason, 1980).

During this period of oppression and turmoil, the people of Korea suffered mainly through lack of freedom of expression. Yet, they did not sit by idly, allowing the political machinations to overcome their freedom to fight for their rights. Although the political grip was tight, underground networks were strong. One of these underground networks took the form of theater. On the outside, above ground, Korean theater performed mostly remakes of Westernized favorites. Furthermore, any scripts that were to be performed had to be passed through the cultural officer in city hall, obviously not a good indication that freedom of expression through literature was going to be appreciated. The underground, theater, however, took the form of numerous artistic expressions of social commentary, mainly criticism of the government, and obviously would never be approved by the cultural officer. Keeping in mind the dictatorial government, such expression was very dangerous and if found out, would invariably lead to incarceration, beatings, or even "accidental" death (Erven, 1992).

These theater performances are called *madang* performances, and through them, information of uprisings was disseminated.

> Madang is very different from Western theatre. It has some resemblance to the dramatic form and treatment of space implied by the term "environmental theater." Its basic scenario changes from venue to venue, adapting to the political particulars wherever it is performed. It may take the form of a festival of people's culture or it may be a mask ceremony. But first and foremost it is rooted in the community of the people, the *kongdong-che*. In the age of modern technology and industrialization, traditional village life and the harmony of nature have been destroyed. It has become difficult for people to express their community spirit. Madang is one attempt to overcome this block. (Erven, 1992, p. 107)

The performances take all forms: dances, paintings, literature/poetry, music, by artists, students, farmers, and workers. Most often, *madang* performances begin with drumming and dancing, with active audience participation. Therefore, on the surface, although listening to the drums may be an awesome and thrilling experience, taking into account the political nature of the history of drumming, much more meaning is involved in the playing of the Korean drums.

Originally, I had wanted to include the political history of the drums in my study, but I realized through my observations of these students that at this university, with this class, there was very little related to the political history of Korea. I must be quick to explain that obviously the history has a great claim in its relationship to the drum class and must not be brushed away as insignificant. Yet I did not feel that it was a strong enough factor with this specific class to emphasize or to come to any conclusions about the students' political nature, but I do feel that it is important enough to mention.

Furthermore, all of the Korean international students are fully aware of the political nature of the *madang* and the drums, as they have lived through political oppression in their education at the universities in Korea; not all may have participated in overt protests, however. Up until the last few years, the government had still been dictatorial, and openly admitting to participating in student protests would have been a foolhardy act. This justified paranoia made me hesitant to boldly ask the students what stand (if any) they had taken in Korea in the *madang* performances. The first-generation Korean students, who are more in touch with the political oppression in Korea, but as permanent residents of the United States are less likely to receive negative repercussions, informed me that the original members of the drum class had been more political in their stands in the performances. With the lessening of political oppression in Korea, the intensity of social and political change has decreased. One particularly well-informed first-generation undergraduate male explained that there is a vast difference between the new class members and the few older members who are still involved. In the first place, most of the original members had attained their degrees and returned to Korea, to be replaced by a new group who now performed for less intense political reasons. In fact, to him, the performances were more culturally informative than politically informative. Now, the drums were used to show the cultural side of Korea, and the political side was drastically underplayed. Perhaps the intensity is diminished, in that the performances are no longer taut with the danger of political repercussions, but I feel it is still important to teach the political history of Korea in order to inform those who are unaware.

To tighten my research into several cohesive threads, I chose to narrow my study to three interrelated areas: race and gender, with culture holding an inseparable influence on both. In the next section, I attempt to make the distinction among the definitions and attributes of Koreans, Korean Americans, and Whites — I had discovered from my observations and to some extent from my own personal experience. Then I delineate the gender division I had noted; and throughout, I show the immutable effect of culture on race and gender.

Race and Culture

Min is a petite, introspective, insightful, second-generation graduate student, who, despite her lack of actual physical connection with Korea, feels a strong connection with her cultural roots. My observation is that perhaps the fact that she is a second-generation Korean American actually reinforces her strong connection with Korea and Koreans. She does not take her roots for granted as many do, and actively searches to learn more about her race and culture at a personal as well as at an intellectual level. She knows more about the history of Korea and shows more awareness of the political and economic situation there than some students directly from Korea, and especially more than other Korean American immigrants in the university. In my interview with her, she was very eager to highlight historical moments in Korea's history. She seemed to establish a close affinity with me because I, myself, am Korean American. She even went so far as to flatter me and called me a "sister."

Among the other students, she is different in that she, along with the one Asian Indian female and one White female, does not speak Korean. Yet she is easily accepted as "Korean." Before my experience with this group, I had thought that being Korean was being Korean, but there is a strong distinction among Koreans directly from Korea, first-generation Korean immigrants, the 1.5 generation, the second generation, and so on. From conversations that I had overheard, there are different traits that are attributed to each group. Furthermore, the various groups regard each other differently. For example, the Koreans directly from Korea seem to hold a somewhat condescending attitude toward the various generations of Korean Americans because they are not quite Korean enough. Yet Min seemed to be an exception to the rule. One Korean male student generously pointed out that although Min was "American," she was still "Korean." He remarked on how she was not as "White" as other Korean Americans.

There is obviously a wealth of meaning in being Korean, Korean American, and White. Koreans from Korea seem to believe that even if one is first generation or 1.5, one is not fully Korean. Therefore, Korean Americans are deficient in some ways and the American part of the Korean American is the cause of the deficiency. The differentiation is not mean spirited in nature, but indicates a fact that they seem to feel is a natural one. Obviously, the various Koreans and Korean Americans are all Koreans physically, but being Korean is more than looking Korean. For example, when I was first introduced to the group, I noticed that they wanted to make a clear distinction about whether I was Korean or Korean American. I cannot objectively say whether their treatment of me differed according to the distinction, but personally I never took offense at their treatment of me. Some immediately thought I was Korean and spoke in Korean to me, and I spoke as much as I could; but when the conversation became too difficult, I had to admit defeat and explain that my Korean was not very good. Always, without blinking an eye, they would convert to English, and I never felt any criticism emanating from them about my inability to speak fluent Korean, as I had expected.

On the other hand, it was clear that the students in the group seemed to view Min as fully Korean, despite her second-generation status. All of the younger Korean females called her "big sister," and the older Korean males and females looked dotingly on her as their little sister. Initially, I was surprised at their easy acceptance of her, taking into consideration that language in Korea is strongly connected with the culture, and she spoke almost no Korean. In fact, during one gathering, after everyone ate and cleared up the food, they began taking turns singing Korean songs. When it was Min's turn, because she did not know any, she asked if she could read them one of her poems. They enthusiastically agreed, despite the fact that the reading of poetry is far from enmeshed in Korean culture. After she read her poem, everyone showed admiration, and easily moved onto the next person for singing. Despite the variance, there was no uncomfortable pause or any awkward transition. Furthermore, despite the fact that many of the Koreans showed low regard for Korean Americans in their mockery about being more "White" than Korean, for Min the definition was loosened a great deal. This generosity of terms and why she was given such an honor was curious to me.

In observing her behavior, I have noted that Min takes on the role of the Korean woman in social interactions. During an interview with her, I was able to detect quite a sharp distinction in her behavior toward me when we were alone and her behavior when she was with the group. With me, she had an easy, open camaraderie. In the group, she showed clear Korean ways. By Korean ways, I mean that she showed a deference to the older students and especially to Hyung, the teacher. In addition, during social interactions at someone's apartment, she took on the domestic role, and served refreshments, prepared the foods, and overall played hostess.

Although other Korean students did not openly acknowledge what they may have felt was a discrepancy between Min's behavior and her second-generation status, several students did comment that "there was no one else like Min" and that she was *cha-kai*; both of which statements are high praise to give to someone. The first comment shows extreme appreciation for the person, and the second word roughly translates into "a really good person," and then some. If you are *cha-kai*, you are good inside and out, in personality, thought, and behavior. In fact, it falls into the stereotype developed from the era of Confucianism, when the expected mode of behavior in a woman was modesty, purity, generosity, and sacrifice. The first term, that "there was no one else like Min," also stems from Confucianism, in that it is paternalistic in nature. Often, the compliment was given when she did something more than she had to. For example, she would often be able to note when someone was thirsty or needed more food, and she would get it before they asked. Then, the receiver would note with a great deal of satisfaction that there was no one else like Min.

I use Min as an example because the contrast in her behavior with me and with the group portrays most clearly the distinctions that are made in being Korean, Korean American, and White. To me, she appeared to embody both aspects of being Korean, as a Korean from Korea and as a Korean American. Furthermore, I will assert that her behavior did not stem from any pretensions, but rather was the only way she knew how to be Korean. She explained that she felt a deep respect for the Koreans in the drum class, and out of respect, her behavior changed to accommodate them and to ease their comfort.

An interesting anecdote I interject in order to perhaps further clarify the differences in terms, is that when I was in high school, along with many other Korean American friends, we also stigmatized those who were "too White." Those Korean Americans we felt were "selling out," we labeled "bananas" or "Twinkies" depending on which high school you attended. The labels were interchangeable, however; the metaphor was that as a banana or a Twinkie, the person was yellow on the outside but white on the inside. They were obviously derogatory terms.

Thus, even the Korean Americans have their expected mode of behavior toward each other. Korean Americans may speak English with each other and may not be fully aware of all aspects of Korean culture, but they believe that some connections with Koreans and Korea should be maintained. Even Min, as a second-generation Korean student, although born in the United States and technically an American, considers herself first and foremost as Korean. She still sees Korea as her country as it is the country of her forefathers. Although she had not been raised on Korean soil, she told me that her parents raised her in the United States as they would have raised her in Korea. She had never even visited Korea, yet she felt such a close affinity to the country that one could not doubt her Korean antecedents. She easily calls herself Korean American, but only because she was born in the United States. She feels that if one were to overlook the technicality of physical birthplace, she is really Korean.

Gender and Culture

The fact that Min was so eager to establish and maintain Korean roots elevated her Korean American status to a Korean status, from the Korean international students' point of view. Furthermore, although she understood only a little Korean and spoke even less, this "deficiency" was overlooked because her desire and attitude was so strongly Korean; a balance of sorts was established. Moreover, in viewing the behavior of the White female and the Asian Indian female in the group, I assert that for basically the same reasons, the latter female was accepted more readily than the other.

Most often, the Indian female would enter the room quietly, surreptitiously pick up a drum, and sit until class was ready to begin. She was soft-spoken, petite, and rather fragile in appearance. When it was her turn to play in front of everyone, she would easily become flustered, but she tried hard, nonetheless. Given Asian sexist paternalism, it was not difficult for Hyung and the other males to feel a sense of protectiveness toward her. Despite the fact that she did not look Korean at all, her behavior did not deviate far from the expected mode of behavior for a Korean woman, and thus she was accepted. Furthermore, unlike Min, she may not have been consciously behaving in any one way, but her behavior was reinforced by the positive approval that was expressed toward her. When everyone was discussing, in Korean, where to go after class, for her benefit, they would ask her in English if she would like to join them. Most often, she would not join the group, but she declined in such a heartfelt and disappointed manner that no one took offense.

On the other hand, the White female seemed to rub some people the wrong way. First of all, she was unlike the stereotypical ideal Korean woman. She was rather tall, strong looking (far from frail), and did not really bother with make up. Her behavior was brash and her demeanor sometimes overbearing. Despite these negative attributes (negative strictly from a Korean perspective), from my observations of her, I did not determine anything truly bad about her. I felt that much of the group's antagonism toward her was sexist in nature because it stemmed from the fact that she did not exhibit conventional feminine characteristics, nor did she try to. When she had to play her piece in front of everyone else, she did not take on the timid reluctance to be center of attention, but played her piece rather boldly, and rather well, even to my untrained ears. From an American perspective, I would acknowledge that her insistence on being how she wanted to be was admirable; but from a Korean perspective, her complete lack of regard for tradition might be what turned off many of the other Koreans, even the female Koreans. After all, being raised in a sexist society, it is difficult for even the staunchest feminist not to hold even a little internalized sexism.

For Koreans and Korean Americans, there are distinct roles that men and women play. One of the female students, a first-generation Korean American undergraduate, was describing her parents to me, and she explained that although her parents wanted her to have everything, to be an educated, independent woman, the contradictions in their beliefs and actions occurred when they pointed out that they felt that it is a duty for a woman always to look her best, and thus should always wear make up. When she explained this idea, I was then able to understand her almost neurotic concern with her appearance. Previous to this enlightening anecdote, I had wondered why she was always checking her appearance when, in my opinion, she looked perfectly fine. In response to her comment, another female then added, with a great deal of feeling, that the only thing she remembered her mother teaching her was to "sit and look pretty." Again, this little tidbit of information explained a lot of her behavior. Before, I had wondered why she showed moments of great insight and intelligence and then contradictory moments of extremely flaky behavior. For instance, most often, she would giggle emptily and not participate much in the discussions in the social gatherings; but she was insightful enough on my first day of observations, to point out the gender division in the kitchen and the livingroom. Most everyone else had forgotten that I was still observing, but she was able to see the situation as I would see it.

Therefore, with that kind of sexist background prevailing in the group, because the White female paid such little attention to her behavior and went against traditional thinking, the men especially—who do not understand what it is like to experience the brunt of sexism but have been raised with sexist attitudes—felt a slight antagonism toward her. Min pointed out to me that she was married to a Korean man, but during my observations neither the White female nor anyone else in the group mentioned this fact at all. I felt that this piece of information could have been revealing, but as no one else brought up the fact, it would have been much too intrusive to ask her bluntly to tell me about her experiences. I felt it would have been interesting to find out about her husband's attitudes and beliefs on sexism, and his idea of feminine behavior and appearance. Because she rubbed most of the Korean males the wrong way, I found it highly interesting that she was married to a Korean. I could only assume that her husband was very different from the usual Korean male, or that she looked and acted differently around him.

Although Hyung could not find fault with her playing, I did note that his generally paternalistic demeanor hardened slightly around her. When some of the Korean female students became flustered, he would very gently and patiently give them his undivided attention. When they played well, he openly expressed his approval by telling them that they had done a good job or gently teased them about how well they were playing these days. I had initially believed that this student's White status led the normally gentle Hyung to take on a slightly harder tone with her and even be stingy with his praises. After further observations, however, I noticed that with another Korean female, who did not fit the ideal Korean woman stereotype, his harshness also showed. Therefore, I was able to conclude that his different behavior and attitude did not stem from what I had thought was his surprisingly racist attitude toward what was not Korean, but rather stemmed from his sexist ideal of feminine behavior and appearance.

Further reinforcing this sexism, Hyung's behavior toward the males was clearly different from that toward the females. With the males, there was no gentleness, although his patience was still there. The males seemed to be allowed less room for mistakes. Several times, when a male made a mistake, Hyung, along with a couple of other males, would jokingly show their disgust at his lack of coordination and his tin ear until he was able to fix the error he had originally made. The ribbing was always in good fun, and not taken completely seriously, but enough so that the male would determinedly attempt to fix his mistake. Furthermore, if Hyung wanted to speak in front of the class, and a male was talking, he would, in a rather harsh tone, tell him to shut up; but if a female was talking, he would look at her reprovingly, like a naughty child, but would not raise his voice.

The gender division was most evident after the class, during the social gatherings. Most of the time, we met at someone's house, and usually it was a female who volunteered her apartment. I can only hazard a guess that the ones who felt their apartments were clean enough for company would offer their residence, because several times, the same person would offer her place, and some females never offered. Therefore, in this sense, the choice of location seemed to be determined mainly by neatness rather than gender. As the notion of neatness and gender always interested me, I asked a few of the females if they remembered neatness being emphasized in their upbringing. The responses were all the same. It was an issue that they had never even thought about. They had always helped their mothers clean the house, and those with brothers had always picked up after them.

One of the females described an incident when she was babysitting her cousins over Thanksgiving break and the male cousin, who was 7 years old, walked in the door, took off his coat, and dropped it on the floor. She had reprimanded him for his carelessness and demanded that he pick up his coat. He was astounded at this request and flatly refused; thus ensued a power struggle. At 7 years of age, his sexist ideas were firmly entrenched. He was so accustomed to his mother picking up after him that he had no idea that anyone would suggest that he pick up after himself. Eventually, the student won the struggle, not because she convinced her cousin it was his responsibility to pick up after himself but because he was forced to concede to her status as an older cousin, therefore someone he was supposed to obey without question. (Although the latter he did not do.)

Therefore, neatness does not seem to be an issue that is discussed, but is an assumed factor in a Korean female's life. As I did not find a woman in the group who was messy, I—as an established slob—asked my mother how my messiness would be regarded in Korean society. She explained that it would show to other people that I was not raised well. She went so far as to buy into the stereotype and admit that if she had been a "proper" mother, she would have taught me to cook and clean and all the other domestic duties expected of a female. From this information, I would assert that the idea of a neatness is attributed to being a proper Korean woman and is much more important to a Korean society that is still so entrenched in clearly established sexist roles—as opposed to a Western society where the roles are not so clear, undeniably sexist yet struggling to overcome this.

At these social gatherings, almost all the females would usually congregate in the kitchen on coming into the apartment. The entry into the kitchen was rarely a casual trek throughout the apartment that happened to end up in the kitchen. Rather, the females would walk into the apartment and go right into the kitchen. Although I joined them, it was interesting to note that I was usually one of only two or three women who were not busy cleaning, cutting, simmering, etc. There were always, minimally, five or six women preparing something. Meanwhile, the men were in the living room, drinking beer, listening to music, or just conversing. Invariably, one or two men would pop their heads into the kitchen to ask the token question of was there anything they could do. Always, the answer was no. From my experience, however, I had learned that when I asked the women if there was anything that I could do, they would automatically say no to me as well, and even suggest that I join the others in the living room; but if I picked up a knife and helped to peel fruit, for example, they would make room for me at the table. Thus, if the men had acted instead of merely asking, the females might not have refused their help. Sometimes the men would stick around in the kitchen to tease, converse, or nibble on the food, but invariably, shortly afterwards they would leave.

Once, I did notice that a male picked up a knife of his own volition and began cutting the carrots. This action was not necessarily received with fanfare, but one or two of the females hovered slightly and teased him on his skill. Not long afterward, one of the hovering females gently removed the knife and suggested he join the others. He did not protest, and easily enough relinquished his domestic duties. My guess is that the female removed the knife not because he was a male performing a female duty, but because he was a male who was unused to such activity and his clumsiness made her nervous. After that incident, out of curiosity, I asked Min what would have happened if Hyung, the instructor, were to enter the kitchen and help with the duties. She laughed and said that it would not happen, but if it were to, all of the women would immediately protest. Thus, even if he wanted to help, he would not be allowed to, not only because he was male but because as an instructor, he held a higher status. Therefore, sexism in Korean culture is not clear cut, with only a male/female division; the age and social status are included and have a great deal of influence.

This gender division was something that I noted on my own, but nothing was verbally or physically acknowledged. I asked one of the males about the division and he protested my stereotyping and said that he would gladly help in any way he could, but most of the time he was pushed out of the kitchen, and because his male friends were in the living room, he never insisted. Similarly, he asserted that most of the females stayed in the kitchen because their female friends were in the kitchen. Furthermore, when I asked him if his behavior would change around his White friends, he did not understand how I could even ask such a question. He did not see anything wrong in his behavior that he would have to revise according to his various types of friends. He archly claimed that he was always himself.

Therefore, this gender division was accepted blindly, although I cannot say for sure if it was because of sexism or because they had been doing the same activities for so long that the roles were established long ago. In this case, the sexism seems to have stemmed from culture. For example, there were two females who were not quite Korean, but not quite Korean American either, and they would help a little in the kitchen, but much of the time they would be out in the living room with the men. Although they were not as actively involved in the conversation as some of the men, they were not ostracized from the group. They drank their beer, listened to the conversation, and sometimes interjected their own opinions. Moreover, the women in the kitchen did not show any disapproval or even seem to notice that they were out with the men. Not once during my observations did anyone comment on the fact that they were not helping in the kitchen.

Therefore, I assert that the gender division in the kitchen and the livingroom was more a question of comfort zones for the two genders than a result of sexism. Often, the food that the women prepared was delicious, but one must realize that none of it was ever so complicated that half a dozen skilled hands were needed. Because these women were adept at cooking, they automatically zoomed into the area in which they felt most comfortable. Furthermore, the two women in the living room felt that area was *their* comfort zone, and there was no stigma attached to them because they did not help in the kitchen.

CONCLUSION AND POLICY RECOMMENDATIONS

Implicit in the image that all that is White American is superior lies the message that all that is not White American is inferior. It is at this point that problems arise. The United States is structurally infused racism. Laws may change, attempts may even be made to change history, but racism handed down generation after generation goes beyond laws, cover-ups, and logic.

Today, Asian Americans are viewed benevolently, even as models. However, the position is tenuous. As history has shown with Japanese Americans, the group can be held up as model one day and driven into internment camps the next. In times of peace, when Asians are not threatening objects, one must look beyond direct, profane insults to all that is implied.

> [T]here need be no discernible instances of discrimination in order for people of color to feel the impact of racial oppression. Instead, people of color may feel inferior or different because they have come to believe the dominant society's message that they are different and do not belong. The accumulated life experiences of racism have a lasting effect on one's perceptions of and feelings about self and identity which may make those in the oppressed group feel out of place, inadequate, or discriminated against even when no one is presently mistreating them. (Osajima, 1993, p. 82)

Thus, one must look beyond the image of the successful Asian businessperson and the complacent whiz kid. One must look deeply at the structural constructs of socialization, education, educators, and curriculum. One must look beyond the numbers implying economic equality. One must delve into history books, learning not only what they say but also what they do not say. Unless we begin to see differently, the greatest possible threat to Asian Americans, and every group of color, for that matter, is that the status quo of oppression will be sustained and perpetuated.

Most of the changes in policy would be simplistic, even obvious. The following are some simple policy recommendations:

- Analysts of educational policy, in their research, must recognize the heterogeneous nature within the Asian American category.
- Multicultural programs must incorporate the diversity and difference within Asian American cultures and experiences rather than utilizing one culture as representative of the entire population.
- Textbooks, particularly history books, must be redesigned to include the role of Asians in the United States.
- Teacher training programs should include participation in at least one non-White, middle class community center (not necessarily just Asian American), in order to gain a better sense of diverse communities that merely observing and student teaching can provide.
- Popular cultural perceptions of Asian Americans must be expanded beyond the homogeneous stereotypes, beyond scholarly research, particularly in the media, through television, radio, magazines, newspapers, and the like.

None of these recommendations is strenuous or particularly innovative or startling, but with the application of these small suggestions, major changes for the better can occur. Especially in terms of education, Asian American students have the difficult task of trying to live up to impossible expectations, and coping with the bicultural pull, identity conflicts, and negative as well as positive stereotypes. As the case study indicated, there is a culture within a culture that survives tenuously at best. Educational policies must take into consideration the abovementioned factors. The problems and conflicts that face Asian Americans have been quiet thus far, which may be attributed to the small population; but with the rapid increase in population, policies for Asian Americans cannot be overlooked much longer. All educational institutions have to consider the barriers of ethnicity, language, culture, learning, and teaching. It is very unrealistic to expect the students, themselves, to have to make the adjustments independently, while researchers, administrators, educators, and policymakers continue with the fallacy of the "model minority."

REFERENCES

Agbayani, A., & Ching, D. M. (1993). *Asian and Pacific Americans in higher education.* Paper presented at the National Association for Student Personnel Administrators Conference, Boston, MA.

Altbach, P. G., & Lomotey, K. (Eds.). (1991). *The racial crisis in American higher education.* New York: State University of New York Press.

Anzaldua, G. (Ed.). (1990). *Making Face, Making Soul.* San Francisco: Aunt Lute Books.

Asian and Pacific Islander concerns: Report of the study committee. (1987). Washington, DC: National Education Association. Microfiche.

Asian and Pacific Islander population in the United States: March 1991 and 1990. (1992). Washington, DC: U.S. Government Printing Office.

Asian Women United of California. (Eds.). (1989). *Making waves.* Boston: Beacon Press.

Banks, C. (Ed.). (1995). *Handbook of research on multicultural education.* New York: MacMillan Publishing.

Barringer, H. R., Takeuchi, D. T., & Xenos, P. (1995). Education, occupational prestige, and income of Asian Americans. In D. T. Nakanishi & T. Y. Nishida (Eds.), *The Asian American educational Experience: A sourcebook for teachers and students* (pp. 146–164). London: Routledge.

Baumrind, D. (1989). The permanence of change and impermanence of instability. *Human Development, 32*(3:4), 187–195.

Baumrind, D. (1991). The influence of parenting style on adolescent competence and substance use. *Journal of Early Adolescence, 11*(1), 56–95.

Chan, S., & Wang, L. (1991). Racism and the model minority: Asian Americans in higher education. In P. G. Altbach & K. Lomotey (Eds.), *The racial crisis in higher education* (pp. 43–67). Albany: State University of New York Press.

Choy, B. (1979). *Koreans in America.* Chicago: Nelson-Hall.

Chun, K. (1995). The myth of Asian American success and its educational ramifications. In D. T. Nakanishi & T. Y. Nishida (Eds.), *The Asian American educational experience: A sourcebook for teachers and students* (pp. 95–112). London: Routledge.

Chun, K., & Zalokar, N. (1992, February). *Civil rights issues facing Asian Americans in the 1990s.* Washington, DC: United States Commission Civil Rights.

Denzin, N. K. (1989). *Interpretive interactionism*. London: SAGE.

Divoky, D. (1988). The model minority goes to school. *Phi Delta Kappan, 70*(3), 219–222.

Endo, G. T., Della-Piana, G. M., & Kubo, C. (1981). Japanese Americans, pluralism, and the model minority myth. *Theory into Practice, 20*(1), 45–51.

Erven, E. van. (1992). *The playful revolution: Theater and liberation in Asia*. Bloomington and Indianapolis: Indiana University Press.

Escueta, E., & O'Brien, E. (1995). Asian Americans in higher education: Trends and issues. In D. T. Nakanishi T. Y. Nishida, (Eds.), *The Asian American educational experience: A sourcebook for teachers and students* (pp. 259–272). London: Routledge.

Espiritu, Y. L. (1992). *Asian American panethnicity: Bridging institutions and identities*. Philadelphia, PA: Temple University Press.

Fong, C. (1995). "From Margin to Center" (7): Teaching introduction to Asian American studies as a general education requirement. *Journal of General Education, 44*(2), 108–129.

Fraenkel, J. R., & Wallen, N. E. (1996). *How to Design and Evaluate Research in Education*. New York: McGraw-Hill, Inc.

Freeman, H. S. (1993, March). *Parental control of adolescents through family transitions*. Washington, DC: U.S. Department of Education; Madison, WI: National Center on Effective Secondary Schooling; Chicago, IL: Spencer Foundation.

Gold, S. J., & Kibria, N. (1993). Vietnamese refugees and blocked mobility. *Asian and Pacific Migration Journal, 2*(1), 27–56.

Grusky, D. B. (Ed.). (1994). *Social stratification in sociological perspective*. Boulder, CO: Westview Press.

Hartman, J. S., & Askounis, A. C. (1989). Asian American students: Are they really a "model minority"? *School Counselor, 37*(2), 109–112.

Hing, B. O. (1993). *Making and remaking Asian America through immigration policy, 1850–1990*. Stanford, CA: Stanford University Press.

Hodge, J. L., Struckmann, D. K., & Trost. L. D. (1975). *Cultural bases of racism and group oppression*. Berkeley, CA: Two Riders Press.

Hoy, W. K., & Miskel, C. G. (1996). *Educational administration: Theory, research, and practice*. New York: McGraw Hill, Inc.

Hsia, J., & Hirano-Nakanishi, M. (1995). The demographics of diversity: Asian Americans and higher education. In D. T. Nakanishi & T. Y. Nishida, (Eds.), *The Asian American educational experience: A sourcebook for teachers and students* pp. 249–258. London: Routledge.

Hu, A. (1989). Asian Americans: Model minority or double minority? *Amerasia Journal, 15* (1), 243–257.

Hurh, W. M. (1990). *The 1.5 generation phenomenon: A paragon of Korean-American pluralism*. Macomb, IL: Western Illinois University Press.

Hurn, C. (1993). *The limits and possibilities of schooling*. Needham Heights, MA: Allyn and Bacon.

Jaggar, A. M. (1988). *Feminist politics and human nature*. Totowa, NJ: Rowman & Littlefield Publishers, Inc.

Jo, M. H., & Mast, D. D. (1993). Changing images of Asian Americans. *International Journal of Politics, Culture, and Society, 6* (3), 417–442.

Kibria, N. (1996). Not Asian, Black or White? Reflections on South Asian American racial identity. *Amerasia Journal, 22*(2), 77–86.

Kim, B. L. C. (1973). Asian Americans: No model minority. *Social Work, 18*(13), 44–53.

Kim, K. S., & Roemer, M. (1980). *Growth and structural transformation*. Cambridge, MA: Harvard University Press.

Kitano, H. H. L., & Rogers, D. (1988). *Asian Americans: Emerging minorities*. Englewood Cliffs, NJ: Prentice-Hall.

Lee, S. J. (1994). Behind the model minority stereotype: Voices of high-and low-achieving Asian American students. *Anthropology and Education uarterly,25*(4), 413–429.

Lesser, J. H. (1985). Always "outsiders": Asians, naturalization, and the Supreme Court. *Amerasia, 12*(1), 83–100.

Li, V. H. (1988). Asian discrimination: Fact or fiction? *College Board Review, 149* (Fall): 20–30, 32.

Liu, W. T., &. Yu, E. S. H. (1995). Asian American studies. In C. Banks (Ed.), *Handbook of research on multicultural education*, pp. 259264. New York: MacMillan Publishing.

Macaranas, F. M. (1980, April). *Social indicators of education and the model minority thesis*. Paper presented at the National Association for Asian and Pacific American Education, Washington, D.C.

Magner, D. K. (1993). Colleges faulted for not considering differences in Asian-American groups. *Chronicles of Higher Education, 39*(23), A32–A34.

Martinelli, P. C., & Nagasawa, R. (1987). A further test of the model minority thesis: Japanese Americans in a sunbelt state. *Sociological Perspectives, 30*(3), 266–288.

Mason, E. S. (1980). The Economic and social modernization of the Republic of Korea. Cambridge, MA: Harvard University Press.

Min, P. G. (Ed.). (1995). *Asian Americans: Contemporary trends and issues*. London: Sage.

Minh-ha, T. T. (1990). *Not you/like you: Post-colonial women and the interlocking question of identity and difference*. In G. Anzaldua, (Ed.), *Making face, making soul*, (pp. 371–375). San Francisco: Aunt Lute Books.

Nakanishi, D. T. (1995a). A quota on excellence? The Asian American admissions debate. In D. T. Nakanishi & T. Y. Nishida, (Eds.), *The Asian American educational experience: A sourcebook for teachers and students* (pp. 273–284). London: Routledge.

Nakanishi, D. T. (1995b). Asian Pacific Americans and colleges and universities. In C. Banks, (Ed.), *Handbook of research on multicultural education* (pp. 683–695). New York: MacMillan Publishing.

Nakanishi, D. T., & Nishida, T. Y. (Eds). (1995). *The Asian American educational experience: A sourcebook for teachers and students*. London: Routledge.

O'Hare, W. P., & Felt, J. C. (1991). Asian Americans: America's fastest growing minority group. *Population Trends and Public Policy, Number 19*. Washington, DC: Population Reference Bureau, Inc.

Okihiro, G. Y. (Ed.). (1988). *Reflections on shattered windows*. Pullman, WA: Washington State University Press.

Okihiro, G. Y. (1994). *Margins and mainstreams: Asians in American history and culture*. Seattle & London: University of Washington Press.

Okutsu, J. K. (1989). Pedegogic "hegemonicide" and the Asian American student." *Amerasia Journal, 15*(1), 233–242.

Osajima, K. (1988). Asian American as the model minority: An analysis of the popular press image in the 1960s and 1980s. In G. Y. Okihiro, et. al., (Eds.), *Reflections on shattered windows*, (pp. 165–174). Pullman, WA: Washington State University Press.

Osajima, K. (1993). The hidden injuries of race. In L. A. Revilla, G. M. Nomura, S. Wong, & S. Hune, (Eds.), *Bearing dreams, shaping visions: Asian Pacific American perspectives*, (pp. 81–91). Pullman, WA: Washington State University Press.

Pai, Y., Pemberton, D., & Worley, J. (1987). *Findings on Korean-American early adolescents and adolescents*. Kansas City: University of Missouri.

Pang, V. O. (1990). Asian Pacific American children: A diverse and complex population. *The Educational Forum, 55*(1), 49–65.

Revilla, L. A., Nomura, G. M., Wong, S., & Hune, S. (Eds.). (1993). *Bearing dreams, shaping visions: Asian Pacific American perspectives*. Pullman, WA: Washington State University Press.

Schatzman, L., & Strauss, A. L. (1973). *Field research: Strategies for a natural sociology*. Engelwood Cliffs, NJ: Prentice-Hall.

Strouse, J. (1988). Immigration and education policy in the United States. *NABE Journal, 13*(Winter), 113–132.

Sue, S., & Kitano, H. H. L. (1973). Stereotypes as a measure of success. *Journal of Social Issues, 29*(2), 83–98.

Sue, S., & Okazaki, S. (1995). Asian American educational achievements: A phenomenon in search of an explanation. In D. T. Nakanishi & T. Y. Nishida (Eds.), *The Asian American educational experience: A sourcebook for teachers and students* (pp. 133–145). London: Routledge.

Suzuki, B. (1995). Education and socialization of Asian Americans: A revisionist analysis of the "model minority" thesis. In D. T. Nakanishi & T. Y. Nishida (Eds.), *The Asian American educational experience: A sourcebook for teachers and students* (pp. 113–132). London: Routledge.

Takaki, R. (1989). *Strangers from a different shore: A history of Asian Americans.* New York: Penguin Books.

Tajima, R. E. (1989). Lotus blossoms don't bleed: Images of Asian women. In Asian Women United of California (Eds.), *Making waves* (pp. 308–317). Boston: Beacon Press.

Tong, R. (1989). *Feminist thought: A comprehensive introduction.* Boulder, CO: Westview Press.

Ueda, R. (1990). The coolie and the model minority: Reconstructing Asian American history. *Journal of Interdisciplinary History, 20*(1), 117–124.

Wang, L. L. (1995). Meritocracy and diversity in higher education: Discrimination against Asian Americans in the post-Bakke era. In D. T. Nakanishi & T. Y. Nishida, (Eds.), *The Asian American educational experience: A sourcebook for teachers and students* (pp. 285–302). London: Routledge.

Watanabe, Y. (1995). The Nisei as model minority: Self-concept and definition of the American dream. *Multicultural Review, 4*(2), 46–53.

We the American ... Asians. (1993). Washington, DC: U.S. Department of Commerce.

Wong, E. F. (1985). Asian American middleman minority theory: The framework of an American myth. *Journal of Ethnic Studies, 13*(1), 51–88.

Woo, D. (1989). The gap between striving and achieving: The case of Asian American women. In Asian Women United of California (Eds.), *Making waves* (pp. 185–194). Boston: Beacon Press.

Yamato, G. (1990). Something about this subject makes it hard to name. In G. Anzaldua (Ed.), *Making face, making soul* (pp. 20–24). San Francisco: Aunt Lute Books.

Afterword

Arlette Ingram Willis and Betty M. Merchant

The singing of our songs has not been without discord. When we began this book almost 4 years ago, we were a group of women embarking on new careers, some as doctoral students deeply engaged in the dissertation process and others as untenured assistant professors, struggling to meet the demands of the universities in which we worked. As we interacted with one another in the context of the academy, we became increasingly aware of the fact that traditional approaches to research were not serving us well in our efforts to negotiate the multiple issues with which we were dealing as we conducted research among people of color.

In the process of resolving the issues associated with producing this book, we have learned to reach out to each other, to trust our own voices, and to persist in our efforts to respect and understand each other. What has come out of our work together is an increased appreciation for the complexity of the research process and the importance of conveying this complexity in our teaching as well as in our writing. Most importantly, perhaps, we have learned that compassion is an essential ingredient for understanding others and ourselves, and for working together for meaningful social change.

Unlike other books written by women and people of color that compare and contrast their approaches to notions of domination, normativity, and objectivity along traditional lines of research, this book uses alternative standpoints that attempt to reestablish the links between researcher and participants. We begin by embracing broader notions of researcher and participants than are typically sheltered under insider/outsider and center–periphery models. We find that the use of such bounded notions leads to dispirited interpretations that fail to acknowledge the inseparableness of race, class, and gendered ways of knowing.

Holistically, the book serves as a large narrative in which the separate chapters exist as metanarratives for the most part. The chapters address issues of identity, methodology, and interpretation by extending the dimensions of culture, race, gender, class, language, and religion beyond "cultural exceptionalism" (McCarthy, 1998, p. xii) to include snippets of our multiple, complex, and interwoven worlds and communities. We use the word "snippets" to acknowledge that the best we can offer is a portion of the multiple realities of our lives and the lives of our participants. Their essence exists, but not within this text. We have attempted to capture and reveal our explicit cultural and personal ways of knowing and viewing the world. Each author embraces the participants, honors the culture, and accepts ethical responsibility to give back to the community.

Cameron McCarthy (1998) warns, and we agree, that

> one of the limitations in current post colonial theory and methodology regarding the analysis of racial identity and center–periphery relations … is the failure of proponents to account for the conditions of production of their own intellectual work and their contradictory interests and affiliations. (p. 5)

The contributing authors identify their cultural affiliations and describe their intellectual development. We believe it is necessary to embrace cultural, familial, and gendered ways of knowing as important and legitimate sources of knowledge that influence our research. There are questions that are left unanswered, which we view as positive. The unanswered questions and the unasked questions may help to point the direction for future study. We turn to the participants to confirm, or disconfirm, our understandings of the data and our interpretations. Traditional notions of reliability are disrupted, as we do not seek confirmation by other independent researchers but rather an understanding of the realities of our participants and the potential for social change.

Distinctive themes emerging from among the chapters include cultural and self-identity, relationships with participants, and the use of narrative as a vehicle for sharing the results. Each author has positioned herself as a cultural being who unashamedly acknowledges that she brings that information into her research. Mehra in her chapter (p. 70) quotes from Denzin (1989) "Interpretive research begins and ends with the biography and self of the researcher" (p. 12). The multiple identities that each of the authors embraces go beyond notions of culture to include dimensions of race, class, gender, language, and religion. The authors have passionately written about the tension they experience within their minds, hearts, and souls as they conduct research as insider/outsider/within. Each author finds herself writing the unwritten as she describes her experiences and processes. Chaudhry believes in the importance of extending research beyond "Eurocentric binarism, whereby the 'objective' is privileged over the 'subjective' (p. 40). Her chapter is notable for the latitude it affords the researcher as she expresses her thoughts, doubts, emotions, and actions.

Merchant explores the challenges that arise in conjunction with conducting research as an "outsider" to the community she is interested in, as well as the issues that are associated with her supervision of a graduate student who is a member of the ethnic community being studied. Henry points out that "one cannot unproblematically assume commonality on the basis of class, culture, gender or any other socio-historico-political dimensions" (p. 7). Kim's chapter portrays the unsettling discontinuities she experiences when conducting research among students who are of the same ethnicity as she, but whose cultural socialization differs markedly from hers.

Mindful of the fact that she is also fulfilling her goals and learning to write for an academic audience, each writer takes her own position as she struggles to fulfill her commitment to self and community as well as her commitment to academia. Willis's chapter provides a powerful narrative of the ways in which she has adapted African American feminist and womanist epistemologies in research. It offers insights into the juncture between romanticized theoretical notions and the realities of fieldwork. Like many of the chapters, it makes clear some of the metacultural messages that are often at work when people of color engage in research within their own communities.

The authors are frank about their relationships with their research participants, and seek to find a space for bridging their participants, and their own cultural ways of knowing. Although each author brings cultural and academic knowledge to her research site, each is committed to viewing the research participants as the experts in their community. For example, Mehra looks to the Asian Indian parents of the children in her study, Henry looks to the African-Caribbean teachers, and Enos looks to the Pueblo leaders. The authors attempt to cross the traditional barriers between community members and researcher by including community members in the research process and creating spaces for their participation, dialogue, and engagement.

In addition, the authors bring and call on, whether consciously or unconsciously, their intimate knowledge of the beliefs, values, and customs, of their community, understood locally and globally. Each author acknowledges that there is a tension in her growing understanding of conducting qualitative research in education, and confesses to wanting to capture the essence of her participants, understanding that it is impossible, and perhaps undesirable, to do so.

Enos emphasizes that her emerging paradigms and perspectives are rooted in ancient and traditional Pueblo life. She uses extensive descriptions of cultural conditions of knowing as she writes:

> Pueblo people acknowledge that subjective ways of knowing are valuable (and, in fact, that humans beings are not—and should not be—objective); that multiple, sometimes even contradictory, viewpoints are possible and what is true may vary from person to person, from culture to culture; that the stories people tell have multiple levels of meaning and each time these stories are told new knowledge is gained. (p. 84)

Under these conditions and within these contexts, culture and language serve not as a colorful background, but as an active medium that communicates meanings and understandings which often move beyond words and descriptions of actions.

A related theme is the importance of family and community. Each author describes a commitment to her family and the larger communities of which she is a part. In addition, each researcher articulates the importance of returning to the community something of her research efforts—giving back, if you will, to those who have supported her efforts. It is never an "I" but always a "we." Zurita writes compellingly of her commitment to improving the academic and social conditions of the Mexican students who are the focus of her research, and in the process, reveals the wrenching personal conflicts she experienced in trying to effect these changes. Each author's personal identity is part and parcel of how she views herself within and outside of the community. Clearly, each brings cultural insider information, some of which cannot be translated into words. They walk along the thin and sometimes invisible continuum from intimate cultural insider to outsider/researcher. In addition, they are careful to share only information that the community deems transmittable to outsiders. The emotions, fears, and dreams that are caught in the glimmer of eyes, the near-silent sighs, and the smiles of quiet recognition evoke what Enos refers to as a belonging to the community.

The narratives and metanarratives of this book form a coherent whole that functions as a transmitter of self, culture, metaculture, and community. The book artfully weaves together a larger conversation and invites readers to join their voices with ours in singing songs for recalling the past, altering the present, and transforming the future.

REFERENCES

Denzin, N. K. (1989). *Interpretive interactonism*. Newbury Park, CA: Sage.
McCarthy, C. (1998). *The uses of culture: Education and the limits of ethnic affiliation*. New York: Routledge.

Author Index

139

Subject Index

P

Pueblo life, 83–85, 88, 90–91, 93, 95, 138
   commitment to community, 92–100
   Pueblo identity, 85, 93–100

R

Research ethics, 47
Researcher identity, 3–4, 21–22, 33–40, 43,
         61–62, 69–75, 86–87, 116 (See also
         Feminist research, Pakistani Muslim
         researcher)
   gender, 33–35, 40–41, 49–54
   multiple identities, 14–15, 17, 34–35, 64, 84
   personal dilemmas, 14–17, 28–31, 35–40,
         77–81, 100
   positionality, 13–14, 17, 70–77 (See also
         Asian Indian)
   race/ethnicity, 3, 5, 6, 8–9, 14–16, 19,
         21–31, 34–40, 43, 49–54, 58–59,

         61–62, 67, 71–82, 84, 86,
         88–92, 100 (See also African
         American)
   religion, 3, 34–37, 40, 44, 51
Researcher relationships, 2–10, 14–17, 22–31,
         34–35, 47, 53, 65–66, 79–82
   researcher—friend dilemma, 26–28, 79–80

S

Subjectivity, 13–14, 28–31, 35, 40–41, 64–67,
         70–71, 74–75, 79, 81, 84, 90–92
   intersubjectivity, 64–67

W

Womanist thought, 46–48

List of Contributors

Lubna Nazir Chaudhry is currently on leave from the University of Georgia, Athens, where she holds a joint position in Women's Studies and the Social Foundations of Education. She is at present conducting ethnographic research in Southern Punjab, Pakistan, on people's perceptions of the relationship between education and development.

Anya Dozier Enos is an enrolled member of Santa Clara Pueblo where she lives with her husband, Terry, and daughters Pasquala and Lisa.. Dr. Enos's research interests include uncovering appropriate research methodology for use with identifying issues in American Indian education.

Annette Henry is associate professor in the College of Education at the University of Illinois at Chicago. Interested in race, gender, culture, language, and equity, she conducts research and writes in three major areas: (a) the epistemology and practice of Black female teachers; (b) the academic achievement and learning of Black female students; and (c) the applications of feminist ethnographic methodologies in educational research especially in multiracial settings.

Judy HeeSung Kim is a Postdoctoral Research Associate at the Institute of Government and Public Affairs at the University of Illinois at Urbana-Champaign (UIUC). She received her doctorate at UIUC from the Department of Educational Policy Studies. Her research interests focus on the multiple intersections of race, gender, and class, Asian Americans in education, feminism for women of color, domestic violence, evaluation and policy analysis.

Beloo Mehra received her PhD in Education in 1998 from the University of Illinois at Urbana-Champaign. Her teaching and research interests include: school-community relations, education of minorities, multicultural education, qualitative research, subjectivity in research and knowledge construction, and action research. She is currently teaching at The McGregor School of Antioch University in Ohio.

Betty M. Merchant is an associate professor In the College of Education at the University of Illinois, Urbana-Chapaign, where she teaches courses in educational leadership, political and social contexts of schooling, educational research, and social change. Her research focuses on educational policy, equity, student diversity, and school leadership. She has taught in public schools, preschool through high school, and in tribally controlled, Native American schools in the southwest.

Arlette Ingram Willis received her PhD from the Ohio State University. She is currently an associate professor at the University of Illinois at Urbana-Champaign. Her research interests include the history of reading research in the United States, sociohistorical foundations of literacy, and teaching/learning multicultural literature for Grades 6 through 12. Among her publications are: *Teaching and Using Multicultural Literature in Grades 9 through 12: Moving Beyond the Canon*, and numerous articles in *Reading Research Quarterly, Language Arts*, and *Harvard Educational Review.*

Martha Zurita is currently a Postdoctoral Fellow at the University of Minnesota, Twin Cities, in the Department of Educational Policy and Administration. Her academic training is rooted in the sociology of education with an emphasis in educational inequities in general and Latina/o education in particular.